# MAXIMUM
# FEASIBLE
# MISUNDERSTANDING

THE CLARKE A. SANFORD LECTURES
ON LOCAL GOVERNMENT AND COMMUNITY LIFE

*A recipe for violence: Promise a lot; deliver a little. Lead people to believe they will be much better off, but let there be no dramatic improvement. Try a variety of small programs, each interesting but marginal in impact and severely underfinanced. Avoid any attempted solution remotely comparable in size to the dimensions of the problem you are trying to solve. Have middle-class civil servants hire upper-class student radicals to use lower-class Negroes as a battering ram against the existing local political systems; then complain that people are going around disrupting things and chastise local politicians for not cooperating with those out to do them in. Get some poor people involved in local decision-making, only to discover that there is not enough at stake to be worth bothering about. Feel guilty about what has happened to black people; tell them you are surprised they have not revolted before; express shock and dismay when they follow your advice. Go in for a little force, just enough to anger, not enough to discourage. Feel guilty again; say you are surprised that worse has not happened. Alternate with a little suppression. Mix well, apply a match, and run. . . .*

— Aaron Wildavsky

*Daniel P. Moynihan*

# *MAXIMUM FEASIBLE MISUNDERSTANDING*

*Community Action
in the War on Poverty*

*AN ARKVILLE PRESS BOOK*

THE FREE PRESS, *New York*
COLLIER-MACMILLAN LIMITED, *London*

# FOREWORD

Clarke A. Sanford of Margaretville, New York, sought to make local government more effective so that it could be responsive to human needs. Being oriented to the solution of human problems, he worked to make local government competent to this task. Equally important to him was the need to be solicitous of individual rights and liberties.

The columns of *The Catskill Mountain News*, which he edited and published for sixty years, were used not only to urge local governments to modernize, but to encourage Federal and state governments really to apply "creative federalism" all the way down to the local level. Having served as mayor of his small upstate New York village and as a member of numerous governmental and voluntary local, regional and national boards, he fully appreciated the necessity and desirability of utilizing modern technology and methods to enrich the quality of rural life.

*The Clarke A. Sanford Lectures on Local Government and Community Life,* established at the State University Agricultural and Technical College at Delhi, New York, by his son, Roswell Sanford, and by his close friend, Armand G. Erpf, a senior partner of Loeb, Rhoades and Company, New York, will over the years encourage and promote scholarship and research in broad areas of local government and community life. This volume by Daniel P. Moynihan is the first of what will be a continuing series of books growing out of the Sanford Lectures. Each, we hope, will be a significant contribution to social science.

When Dr. Moynihan delivered the annual Clarke A. Sanford Lecture at the State University Agricultural and Technical College at Delhi, New York, in 1967, he discussed the "war on poverty." Since that time, events have unfortunately confirmed his view, which he has elaborated in this book.

Many of us who shared in the formation and the running of local community action agencies have been both frustrated and dismayed. What was to have been a "grass roots" war on poverty, sensitive and responsive to local need, emerged instead as a rigid program, directed all too frequently by inexperienced and arrogant bureaucrats who couldn't care less about local conditions and problems.

Why has the poverty program fallen so short of its goal? What went wrong? In the following pages, Dr. Moynihan provides a significant part of the answer. While some may take exception to his conclusions, others, like myself, having experienced the ordeal, will find themselves in substantial agreement. More important, however, is the lesson Dr. Moynihan contends social science must consider if we are to profit from this ill-fated experience. To avoid similar pitfalls, social scientists must have more reliable data before advocating and insisting upon the adaption of theoretical solutions for social and economic ills. Tampering with the social and political processes without adequate objective data, as we have witnessed in the case of the poverty program, often leads to disastrous results.

*Seldon M. Kruger*
PROFESSOR AND CHAIRMAN
GENERAL STUDIES DIVISION
STATE UNIVERSITY AGRICULTURAL AND
TECHNICAL COLLEGE AT DELHI, NEW YORK

# PREFACE

This essay was originally prepared as the Clarke A. Sanford Lecture on Local Government and Community Life and delivered at the Delhi Agricultural and Technical College of the State University of New York in the late spring of 1967. Although at that time the course of events leading to a downgrading of the community action programs of the "war on poverty" seemed already set—a theme of the lecture having been the near inevitability of this development, given the flawed beginnings of the program—a measure of prudence suggested that a published version await the final action of Congress on the Economic Opportunity Act of 1967. In a limited sense it can be said there was no need for such caution. Events proceeded much as could have been, and in this case was, anticipated.

(Political scientists, like politicians, can occasionally discern the unavoidable when it is not too far ahead in the fog.) In a different perspective, however, the year that has intervened from the first to the present version of the manuscript has added a dimension of symbolic significance to this subject that may enhance its interest.

My subject is the origin, nature, and internal contradictions of a great national effort at social change conceived under the administration of John F. Kennedy and brought to fruition under that of Lyndon B. Johnson. When I first took it up, that effort seemed faltering, but the administration itself seemed securely in power, and the national initiatives begun in the early 1960's seemed likely to persist for something like their appointed time. But within twelve months it all had ended. The President had, in effect, resigned his office, giving as his reason the belief that his continued presence would only enhance the divisiveness and rising level of internal conflict that characterized the times. An administration that hardly months earlier had held out, and genuinely believed in, the prospect of unprecedented national consensus, a twentieth century era of good feeling that would heal at last some of the most serious of the many wounds that the American peoples have inflicted on one another in the course of forming the nation, was forced to leave office before further, more grievous—some would even predict fatal—injury was done. In the language of continental politics, the regime was toppled. Nothing quite like this had ever occurred in American history.

An incident in the spring of 1968 summed matters up. Seeking to attend the funeral of the Cardinal Archbishop of New York, the President of the United States was forced to slip into St. Patrick's Cathedral by a back door, in the manner of a medieval felon fleeing to sanctuary, save that it was not the authorities, but an outraged element of the people whom the President fled. Clearly at the national level the quest for consensus had failed.

Clearly it had failed also at the level of local affairs. The seven-year span that had seen the establishment of community action programs in over one thousand American cities (and in some rural areas) had witnessed also a rise of internal conflict and violence that in truth was without precedent in American experience. (The labor violence of the 1870's and 1930's was never so widespread. In the nineteenth century, urban turbulence in the form of street fighting and crime was general enough, but had no symbolic or ideological coherence. The Civil War was, in truth, what the South continues to call it, a War Between the States, that is to say between organized and disciplined polities in which internal dissent was largely confined to accepted political processes.) Crime, presumedly one of the first signs of a deteriorating community, was very probably rising during this period, and the public perception of it was rising even faster. Rioting by urban Negroes became endemic, starting in New York the nation's cultural capital, in the summer of 1963, and reaching the political capital in Washington four years later. Political assassination became an ominous political problem, directed first to Negro civil rights leaders, next to the Presidency itself, and then by a process of diffusion to politically active or symbolic persons generally. The heft of it would seem to be that the events of a decade that had begun with the utmost promise that America, one of the few, one of the oldest, and incomparably the most powerful of the world democracies, would grow in strength and internal cohesion and was likely at any moment, indeed, to be suffused with a spirit of enterprise and daring such that history would look to it as a golden age, the events of that decade had progressed from vision to nightmare. The great Republic had—incredibly, monstrously—been brought to the point of instability.

It is not yet clear whether we shall once again take charge of events as it seemed for a moment we were doing. (Or if that is never more than illusion, whether things in some random fashion will simply start to go our way again.) But surely it is the responsibility of those who would take part in those events to try to understand them. Not, as Sydney Smith would have said, with any very great expectation of success, but rather as a kind of moral discipline. Who would hope in any final or even intermediary sense to understand politics, which is to say to understand men? What one can hope for, however, is that in the day-to-day life of politics those wielding power will seek to *think* as best they can about the events in which they are caught up. That is to say, that they will be serious about assembling such facts as can be had, will compare them with what, if anything, is known of the past, will consider likely events of the future, and, above all, will try to be clear in their own meaning and will seek to understand clearly the meaning of others. This will seem an observation of almost daring banality to some, but after fifteen years of involvement in or with local, state, and national government, I must say that these are qualities more rare than they need be, and perhaps especially so among liberals intent on desirable social change. Wishing so many things so, we all too readily come to think them not only possible, which very likely they are, but also near at hand, which is seldom the case. We constantly underestimate difficulties, overpromise results, and avoid any evidence of incompatibility and conflict, thus repeatedly creating the conditions of failure out of a desperate desire for success. More than a weakness, in the conditions of the present time it has the potential of a fatal flaw.

I believe that this danger has been compounded by the increasing introduction into politics and government of ideas originating in the social sciences which promise to bring about social change through the manipulation of what might be termed the hidden processes of society. That is to say, the manipulation of those systemic relations between one set of activities and another which are not normally perceived by the participants as being related, but which on closer examination are seen to be. The discovery and analysis of such relationships is the very essence of the social sciences. Yet it remains an occult art. And a highly uncertain one. Not long ago it could be agreed that politics was the business of who gets what, when, where, how. It is now more than that. It has become a process that also deliberately seeks to effect such outcomes as who *thinks* what, who *acts* when, who *lives* where, who *feels* how. That this description no more than defines a totalitarian society is obvious enough. But it has come to characterize democratic government as well. I do not resist this development; I would seek only to identify it, and to suggest some of the rules of conduct that probably ought to guide us in carrying forth such activities. As my example, I turn to the ill-fated community action programs of the war on poverty. The term "ill-fated" implies a judgment, and that is precisely what I offer: to wit, that the program was carried out in such a way as to produce a minimum of the social change its sponsors desired, and bring about a maximum increase in the opposition to such change, of the kind they feared. This is a large load of conclusion for a slight work of this kind to bear, and it is perhaps best that, in the manner of more rigorous social scientists, I state at the outset something of my methodology so that readers in turn can judge with what degree of confidence my assertions are to be entertained. As will be seen, there is a further danger of personal bias of which the reader will want also to know.

To a considerable degree, this is a personal memoir growing out of experiences in the U. S. Department of Labor during the period 1961–65. Having earlier, while on the staff of Governor Averell Harriman of New York, become involved with questions of crime and delinquency (and having acquired a deep regard for the work of Lloyd Ohlin), I readily enough became interested in the work of the committee President Kennedy established on that subject, of which the Secretary of Labor was a member. I later became involved with the abortive planning for a domestic Peace Corps that began in 1962. Still later, as economic growth resumed during those years, and unemployment became less and less macroeconomic in nature, I grew more and more involved with issues of "hard core" poverty—the situation of those persons in the population whose life circumstances do not appear to respond, at least very quickly, to the large movements of the economy. When in October 1963 President Kennedy decided that "a basic attack on the problems of poverty and waste of human resources" would be a central feature of the 1964 legislative program, in the routine course of events (I was then Assistant Secretary of Labor for Policy Planning and Research) I became a member of the group convened by Walter H. Heller, Chairman of the Council of Economic Advisors, to draw up such a program. As is well known, this process was given the greatest priority in the immediate aftermath of the Kennedy assassination. A number of accounts of the events that followed have been written, most notably that of James L. Sund-quist (who was also an active participant), and there is no need for any of it to be repeated here, save to record my impression of one development that affected my judgment of community action then, and to some degree continues to do so.

The matter comes to this: the position of the Department of Labor at the time was that the most important measure that could be taken to combat poverty was a more or less massive employment program. Our first priority was the enactment of the "Youth Employment Act," then S. 1. The position of the Council of Economic Advisors and of the Bureau of the Budget, however, was that the entire antipoverty program should be subsumed under a set of "community action programs." Dutifully, I pressed against this position for no better reason than that it was not that of the Department of Labor. My impression, almost certainly exaggerated but not, I think, entirely unfounded, is that this opposition, which took the usual variety of forms, helped produce the December 1963 stalemate in the planning of the program, a stalemate Theodore Sorensen could not or would not resolve, which led President Johnson to call in Sargent Shriver, a completely neutral party, to impose some order on the warring principalities that are sometimes known as the Federal government. In the manner of the peacemaker, Shriver assembled representatives of the principal positions; I was asked to join the task force which thereupon drew up the Economic Opportunity Act of 1964. Shriver's approach, the logical one, was to adopt some portion, at least, of everyone's program. The result, as I have elsewhere written, was "not a choice among policies so much as a collection of them." The Labor Department's employment program became Title I of the bill. The Budget Bureau's community action programs became Title II. And so on. The first draft of the bill was prepared by Assistant Attorney General Norbert A. Schlei after a task force meeting of February 23rd. In virtually the exact language of the final act, it provided that a "Community Action Organization" meant one "which is developed and conducted with the maximum feasible participation of the residents of the areas" that were involved. No one seems to recall for certain just who was responsible for the phrase. My recollection is that it was Frank Mankiewicz (it is clearly a lawyer's term), although it could as well have been Schlei's taking the sense of the meeting. Mankiewicz recalls that it emerged from the same session in which he, I, Harold Horowitz, and John Steadman took part. Adam Yarmolinsky recalls the phrase as having originated with Richard W. Boone, and certainly Boone insisted on the principle. And this is the point: "maximum feasible participation" was to some of those involved in the war on poverty considerably more than a slogan, in the sense that "war on poverty" itself was really no more than one of Richard N. Goodwin's magic phrases. Community action with citizen participation was a coherent and powerful idea working its way into national policy, albeit little noticed or understood at the time.

The bill proceeded through several drafts. Shriver in the meantime presented it in outline to the cabinet, where what appears in retrospect to have been a fateful decision was made, of which more later. Yarmolinsky and I accompanied him to the cabinet meeting and a month later, on March 16th, sat on either side of him as he presented the measure to the opening session of the hearings held by the House Committee on Education and Labor.

There my personal involvement in these events

ended. Yarmolinsky, who had been Shriver's second-in-command throughout, stayed on in his position. I returned immediately to the Department of Labor, and thereafter (interagency jealousies having grown instantly acute) felt it wise to stay away from the task force almost completely. Save for an invitation to the bill-signing ceremony in August (I went through the line twice and picked up a pen for Michael Harrington), my involvement with and knowledge of events that occurred thereafter is almost entirely second hand. In this essay, for details of the planning process that went went on in the summer and fall of 1964, I rely most heavily on the remarkable Harvard senior thesis, prepared from primary sources, by Richard Blumenthal. (And, as any student of community action, I am everywhere indebted to *Dilemmas of Social Reform* by Peter Marris and Martin Rein.)

In July 1965, I left Washington, and having come to be regarded as a friend of Robert F. Kennedy, my access to knowledge of the workings of the poverty program was thereafter little greater than that of any other citizen. Possibly less, as a process of exclusion ensued that any who have been in, and then out, of favor in Washington will recognize.

I retained, however, a considerable interest in the progress of the community action programs. This interest had been heightened by developments in the Mobilization for Youth program in New York City, which, during the late spring of 1964, got in trouble over alleged (and nonexistent) subversive infiltration. At that time, still in the government, I began to feel that official Washington had an entirely different, almost antithetical view of the style and function of "community action" from that of its proponents in the field, and that the intermediaries who had transmitted the idea, were either unaware of this discrepancy, or if aware not perhaps entirely candid about it. It seemed to me inevitable that unless the apparent fact of these two quite different views of community action was confronted, a good deal of bitterness and confusion was likely to follow. On further reflection I perceived what appeared to be a third concept of community action, and then, considering the task force approach, yet a fourth. I grew seriously concerned: if the role of political executives is not infrequently to confuse things in public, just as often it is to attempt to clarify them in private. In mid-1964 I sought and obtained audiences with men of influence and stated the case. I argued that the Bureau of the Budget understanding of what the community action programs was going to be like was probably not what OEO was thinking, and almost certainly not what was going to happen, regardless of the wishes of anyone in Washington. It did not follow that a choice had to be made between the divergent views, but I pleaded that the parties involved had to get clear with one another that they were thinking of different things. Without exception those to whom I spoke were kind but uncomprehending. Or so at least I thought. (They may have known perfectly well what was going on, but for sufficient reasons were reluctant to interfere.) At all events, my intervention changed nothing. Save for me personally. I acquired—I feel it important to be absolutely open on this point—a limited but real enough intellectual stake in seeing what I felt to be the internal contradictions in the program come into the open. My warnings, marginal and futile as they were, would nonetheless have been vindicated. A not unfamiliar theme in memoirs of government service!

In the fall of 1966 I published a brief note in *The Public Interest* expounding these contradictions and forecasting trouble, although by this time trouble had already largely come to pass. In the spring of 1967 I expanded further on the subject in the Sanford Lecture at Delhi, and now, a year later, do so one last time. The narration that follows is as objective an account as I have been able to write; because of the fear of a personal bias it may indeed be more so than would normally be the case. If it may be that I anticipated some of the troubles that befell the program, I hope it will be also clear that I took not the least pleasure in them. To the contrary, to see an effort begun with such great hopes remorselessly dismantled, is to know a disappointment not easily got over.

There is, of course, at this moment a sense of an even larger drama having ended. As I write I am just returned from the funeral of Robert F. Kennedy. It was not in any sense a triumph, as in a way his brother's funeral had been a triumph. It was, rather, a long, desolate, remorseless demonstration of defeat. We lost. The momentary generosity of our enemies is compounded primarily of that knowledge. The "we" includes many people, but to an intensive degree it includes those whose names will appear in this narrative. By and large they had scattered in the ineluctable diaspora that followed the assassination of John F. Kennedy. Now they had gathered to accompany his brother to that slight knoll in Arlington cemetery near the eternal flame that in warning and reproach gleams across Memorial Bridge to the sacred precincts of the city.

Hackett, Mankiewicz, Boone, Yarmolinsky, Shriver, Heller, Schlei, Galbraith, Goodwin, Moyers. Others like them. Not a pantheon perhaps, but a list of men who hoped much for their country, but whose hopes for this moment, at least, seemed to have come to little more than the burial by moonlight of a leader who in the face of setback and disappointment did not lower, but did indeed raise, *his* expectations for that country. In a curious sense community action is an idea that came more and more to be associated with Robert F. Kennedy, even as he grew further removed from the centers of power in Washington where (such being the irony of things) its official fate was determined. If there be those who feel there is no power in the idea, they would have done well to ride that funeral train and to watch the poor of America standing vigil as his body passed by. For the moment uncertainty is all, reconciliation distant. Yet in the gentleness and endurance of those faces there was all the hope that any nation ought to need, or could expect to have.

> *Agnus Dei, qui tollis peccata mundi,*
> *Dona nobis pacem.*

*D. P. M.*

*Derrymore*
*West Davenport,*
*New York*
*June 11, 1968*

# CONTENTS

# CHAPTER ONE

# THE QUEST
# FOR
# COMMUNITY

No person who has come to know the State of New York can fail to have been intrigued with the rich mixture of place names that tells so much of its history. Names matter, words matter—and in New York State were perhaps especially intended to. Its geography is stamped throughout with claims and counterclaims: some of battles long resolved; others of issues as alive today as when the first town council nailed its politics to the flag pole, and chose to be known as Corinth or Livingston Manor, Franklin or Rennsselaerville, Kingston or Athens. Three themes in particular emerge: the European past; the then frontier present; the democratic future, itself, however, but a revival of an even more ancient past. If Americans can be said to be the first people consistently to locate the happiest age of man in the future rather than the past, it was very much from a sense of history—the classical models of ancient republics gradually fused with a liberal rational belief in progress from one stage of development to another —that they derived the great expectations of the period of exploration and settlement. Homer, Medusa, Palmyra, Ithaca, Cicero, Pharsalia, Pompey, Seneca, Tully, Cincinattus: surely place names based on something more than the whim of surveyors with a smattering of Latin; surely names meant to tell something of the purposes of the men and women who settled there.

If the *Historical Atlas of New York State* is to be relied upon—and given its sure depiction of the backroads of the state, a measure of confidence is warranted—the county seat of Delhi, on the banks of the West Branch of the Delaware River, evokes an especially happy combination of community purpose and pride. It seems there was a Judge Foot in the legislature at the time Delaware County was formed from parts of Ulster and Otsego in 1797. The judge was apparently a man of political power and skill, and had earned from his colleagues the sobriquet of "The Grand Mogul." When he chose to settle at the seat of the new county, the townspeople out of sheer pleasure named their hamlet Delhi, from whence the original Moguls had ruled. In that gesture of harmony between the local power structure—a term one likes to think was not then known—and the popular will, there is to be sensed a community at ease with itself, able to act on the basis of an accord that represented, if not everyone, at least something more than an arithmetical majority, something closer to that preponderance associated with the term *consensus*. There is little need to add that such serenity will have been intermittent and partial at best, much as was democracy in Athens, and obviously is to be treated as an abstraction rather than an historical condition. But neither is it necessary to construct delusions about a nonexistent past in order to perceive that the communities of the American present seem to be in a phase of rising discord, tension, hostility, anger, and even at times violence and disarray. Indeed, some question the American capacity for self-government in the conditions of modern life, and they are welcome to their speculations. But apocalyptic preoccupations aside, it is not unreasonable but necessary to ask whether the level of community competence, to use Leonard Cottrell's term, is any longer adequate to the demands increasingly imposed upon local government, and in particular city government.

If this question has been lurking in the minds of many persons for several decades now, it has been much in the forefront of events since the enactment in 1964 of the Economic Opportunity Act with its singular provision for the establishment, in the poorer neighborhoods of the nation, of community action programs involving the "maximum feasible participation" of the local residents. These were to be, as Sargent Shriver, first director of the Office of Economic Opportunity declared, the corporations of the new social revolution. In the oldest and presumably strongest tradition of American democracy, the local people themselves, those actually caught up in the problem at hand, were to organize themselves to deal with it. The war on poverty, as the Office of Economic Opportunity declared in one of its first publications, and perhaps its only witticism, was to be "A Hometown Fight." And it was to be an epic one. On the morning of August 20, 1964, as President Johnson signed the Act in the Rose Garden of the White House, he declared that "on this occasion the American people and our American system are making history. . . . Today for the first time in the history of the human race, a great nation is able

3

to make and is willing to make a commitment to eradicate poverty among its people." It would be a great program, and it would succeed, he asserted. Probably few persons noted that he also declared it would be a "prudent" one.

Three years later the President was to tell a leading member of the Senate Committee responsible for the antipoverty legislation that although he was prepared to stick with it, this was hardly his favorite program. Clearly it had become anything but. For months on end, no mention of the war on poverty had emerged from the White House. When in March 1967, the administration sent to Congress its proposed Economic Opportunity Act of 1967, the accompanying message spoke only of a "strategy against poverty." The *New York Times* termed the whole episode a "retreat" in a battle that in truth had never really been joined. Others, notably those who had "enlisted for the duration" (such were the hyperboles that had earlier emerged from the press officers of the campaign), used yet harsher terms. At the last possible hour of the 1967 session, in what was regarded as something of a legislative feat, Congress authorized another two years of the program, but only just. In his first weeks in office the President had proposed "unconditional" war on poverty; in short order that whole range of metaphor had become embarrassing if not, indeed, obscene. The survival of the program had been pretty much assured, but its pride of place as the principal social effort of the administration had long since been lost. In the spring of 1968 Shriver was relieved of his command and given the Paris embassy for a high-level taste of what the White House staff, preoccupied by a real war that was not going any better, had come to term "R & R," for Rest and Recuperation. OEO had become just another agency. Few could off hand recall the

name of the career civil servant who succeeded
Shriver. When the battalions (or whatever) of the
Poor People's March began to arrive in Washington
later in the spring they seemed unaware that either
the Office or its director existed.*

In the history of these years, yet to be written, it
will almost certainly be held that it was the war in
Vietnam that made the war on poverty untenable. Vietnam imposed severe strains on the financial resources
of the United States, and given the balance of payments and the gold situation, even threatened the mon-
etary stability of the nation. (In the summer of 1967,
with some of the principal cities of the nation literally
in flames, the Secretary of the Treasury was to inform
the President that there was simply no additional
money to spend on antipoverty measures if the dollar

---

\* No slight is intended Mr. Bertrand M. Harding, a distinguished
career civil servant, for whom anonymity is a mark of professionalism. In the typical career sequence of the bureaucratic élite in Washington, identical in all save its informality to that of the British
Treasury official, Harding, upon entering the government, served
eleven years in the Bureau of the Budget, moving thence to the Internal Revenue Service, where he rose to Deputy Commissioner, a post
he held at the time of his appointment to OEO. He had by then received the Career Service Award of the National Civil Service League,
the Treasury Department Exceptional Service Award, and the Rockefeller Public Service Award (that is, CMG, KCMG, GCMG). He was
never far from the money where he was being passed out or taken in,
until, that is, he was dispatched to take over and bureaucratize an
unruly new agency. Half a year before his appointment I described
this sequence. *Mutatis mutandis*, I believe OEO is following the
pattern:

> "How one wishes," Nathan Glazer writes . . . , "for the open
> field of the New Deal, which was not littered with the car-
> casses of half successful and hardly successful programs,
> each in the hands of a hardening bureaucracy." But the
> pattern persists: the bright idea, the new agency, the White
> House swearing in of the first agency head, the shaky be-
> ginning, the departure 18 months later of the first head,
> replacement by his deputy, the gradual slipping out of sight,
> a Budget Bureau reorganization, a name change, a new
> head, this time from the civil service, and slowly obscurity
> covers all. Who among us today could state with certainty
> exactly what did become of the Area Redevelopment Admin-
> istration, that early, shining creation of the New Frontier?
> (D. P. Moynihan, "The Politics of Stability," The New
> Leader, Oct. 9, 1967, p. 8.)

was to be saved.) The war abroad in any event commandeered the energies of that tiny group of men at the top of the American government who are able to get anything different done. Not less important, the committee structure and membership of the Congress at this time was such that in order to obtain and keep support for the war abroad, the President was required to deal with precisely those members who were least enthusiastic about the domestic campaign. Yet something more than this is involved. From the outset the war on poverty aroused opposition, within the administration itself, within the Congress, and within political circles of the nation broadly conceived, from sources that could have been expected to be most in favor of it. To explain the precipitous decline in what was to have been an extraordinary and prolonged national undertaking, it is necessary to account for this source of opposition as well, and this matter turns on the peculiar history of the community action programs provided by Title II of the Act.

As with most major (or attempted major) social initiatives, the origins of the community action programs of the war on poverty will be found first of all in intellectual history. The record is that of a set of ideas making their way from university lecture rooms and professional journals to the halls of Congress and the statute books of the national government. And in surprisingly short order. That action should originate in thought is nothing unusual, nor is it especially noteworthy, in this or any other time, that this involved the work of professional men pursuing their professions. The speed of the transmission process, however, is apparently new, involving as it would seem to do, the emergence of a professional style in reform also, and of a cadre of persons in and about American government whose profession is just that.[1] These processes, obviously, are closely linked, and very likely interact in some ways, but it is the history of the underlying idea that must be first attended.

People change their minds. This simple observation of Michael Polanyi is in truth a sharp challenge to the incremental model of public opinion slowly making its way up one hill of belief and down another. Often the process is just the opposite. We awake one morning and the world is different. We have changed our minds. What we once believed we no longer believe, and that is all there is to it.

Something of this sort happened to classical liberalism in mid-twentieth century. A set of untroubled, even serene convictions as to the nature of man and society, and the ever more promising prospects of the future, of a sudden collapsed. No one any longer really believed it. Or at least on the growing edge of thought it came to be seen that the nineteenth century faith in secular individualism had simply not worked out, had brought mankind into a zone of disaster from which its eventual emergence was problematic at best. As with any great change in belief, an interaction of prophets and events was at work. Artists and writers had been the first to sound the warning. Then theologians and psychologists. Social scientists followed: somewhat resistant to their findings, but faithful to their standards of evidence when it appeared. Nazi Germany, Stalinist Russia, the War, the Bomb confirmed the prophets, and suddenly, by mid-century, just about everyone who thought about it was convinced the world was in deep trouble, that the liberal rationalist experiment had proved near to catastrophic.

This is not the exaggeration it will at first appear. Few persons think, and fewer still take notice of those who do. But within the limited circles involved there was at mid-century a perceptible and almost precipitous turning from received liberalism. As good a symbol as any was the succession, in the spring of 1951, of Michael Oakeshott to the chair of Harold Laski at the London School of Economics and Political Science. John O'Hara has said that when Benchley died the party was over, and something like that happened with the passing of Laski in 1950. The great expectation that a viable process of social change could emerge from a purposeful, elitist combination of humane feeling and humane letters somehow did not survive him. Oakeshott, an English Hegelian, was not so much a conservative in his desires for society as in his expectations of it. His theme: "The world is the best of all possible worlds, and everything in it is a necessary evil." His expectation was that it would remain so.

Oakeshott's message, in his inaugural lecture, was that the future will be very like the past, and that—perceiving this—the task of governing was to accept it, and in so doing, to draw on what is strongest and best in the necessarily mixed bag of political tradition in order to manage such change as *is* possible. He wrote:

Those societies which retain, in changing circumstances, a lively sense of their own identity and continuity (which are without that hatred of their own experience which makes them desire to efface it), are to be counted fortunate, not because they possess what others lack, but because they have ready mobilized what none is without and all, in fact rely upon.

In political activity, then, men sail a boundless and bottomless sea; there is neither harbour for shelter nor floor for anchorage, neither starting-place nor appointed destination. The enterprise is to keep afloat on an even keel; the sea is both friend and enemy; and the seamanship consists in using the resources of a traditional manner of behavior in order to make a friend of every inimical occasion.

Oakeshott preached the art of the possible, and bespoke the fate of those who reject those limitations:

"to try to do something which is inherently impossible is always a corrupting enterprise."

In the United States at this time rather a different gloss was given the successive disasters of the twentieth century. Less certain of their own political and social traditions, less confident as to just how widely these were shared, American analysts would have settled for a future no worse than the past, but had come to fear there might be no such luck. The New Deal was ending in a kind of generalized disappointment. Nothing better seemed likely to follow. (Nothing did.) A populist anticommunism seemingly bent on linking up with a still virulent streak of right-wing capitalism suggested that the American mass was drifting towards the same condition of hysteria and fear born of insecurity and rootlessness which provided the setting for the onset of totalitarianism in Europe. It was clear that something had gone wrong, and something had to be done about it.

It was also clear, or seemed so, that the problem lay in the erosion of those institutions by which persons in the mass relate to one another on terms that give rise to shared expectations, confidence, and trust. These concerns were summarized in a masterful volume by Robert A. Nisbet, an avowed conservative, published in 1953 under the title, *The Quest for Community*.[2] And this became the master term.

Nisbet's theme is alienation. He begins, paraphrasing Marx: "a specter is haunting the modern mind, the specter of insecurity." He continues: "Surely the outstanding characteristic of contemporary thought on man and society is the preoccupation with personal alienation and cultural disintegration."[3] The nineteenth century, the age of individualism and rationalism, whose key words were "individual," "change," "progress," "reason," and "freedom" were past. The key

9

words of the modern lexicon were "disorganization," "decline," "insecurity," "breakdown," "instability." The rationalist view of man had collapsed.

Nisbet's analysis was a familiar one; the fact of its being widely shared was central to his thesis. The progress of secular liberalism had been one in which the institutions that formally mediated between the individual and the state had gradually eroded, as had relations between individuals. The result was anguished insecurity in the individual, and that in turn led, by a process of the politicization of personal anxiety, to totalitarianism in the state. Despotism, for being benevolent, was not thereby the less despotic.

The contemporary crisis was depicted as first of all one of authority, a very different thing from power. Nisbet writes:[4]

> By authority, I do not mean power. Power, I conceive as something external and based upon force. Authority, on the other hand, is rooted in the statuses, functions, and allegiances which are the components of any association. Authority is indeed indistinguishable from organization, and perhaps the chief means by which organization, and a sense of organization, becomes a part of human personality. Authority, like power, is a form of constraint, but unlike power, it is based ultimately upon the consent of those under it; that is, it is conditional. Power arises only when authority breaks down.

Freedom, he asserts, "lies in the interstices of authority." But how, then, to secure it? Here Nisbet is explicitly and implacably functional. The authority of small groups such as the family, the local community, and other traditional associations had eroded because their functions had eroded. Useless to talk, for example, of the breakdown in family ties: if families have no functions, their ties will not bind. He follows the Hammonds, Ostrogorski, Niebuhr, and others in the analysis of the process whereby Protestantism and capitalism gradually "stripped off the historically grown layers of custom and social membership, leaving only leveled masses of individuals." And with Niebuhr he holds that the civilization that begins by creating this autonomous individual ends by destroying him. This is the key to Nisbet's analysis. Men need a sense of community. It is because that sense had eroded that the *quest* for it had become "the dominant social tendency of the twentieth century." Having no other institutions at hand, men have unavoidably turned to the state to provide this sense, and that has repeatedly and probably necessarily ended in totalitarianism:[5]

> The ominous preoccupation with community revealed by modern thought and mass behavior is a manifestation of certain profound dislocations in the primary associative areas of society. . . . Behind the growing sense of isolation in society, behind the whole quest for community which infuses so many theoretical and practical areas of contemporary life and thought, lies the growing realization that the traditional primary relationships of men have become functionally irrelevant to our State and economy and meaningless to the moral aspirations of individuals. We are forced to the conclusion that a great deal of the peculiar character of contemporary social action comes from the efforts of men to find in large-scale organizations the values of status and security which were formerly gained in the primary associations of family, neighborhood, and church. This is the fact, I believe, that is as revealing of the source of many of our contemporary discontents as it is ominous when the related problems of political freedom and order are considered.

Thus he cites Robert Birley: "The most obvious symptom of the spiritual disease of our civilization is the widespread feeling among men that they have lost all control of their destinies. . . . Hitler's answer to that frustration was one of the main secrets of his power."[6] And of course by this time Bertrand Russell's analysis of Communist Russia as a theocracy was well known.

It will be readily apparent, and was to Nisbet, that in effect he was stating that the conservative thinkers of the nineteenth century had been right after all. Right, for example, in arguing that the crime of the French revolutionaries lay not in the individuals they executed, but in the institutions they destroyed. Right in predicting that in the absence of such institutions secular liberalism would lead to the atomized mass, the alienated individual, and the omnipotent state. Burke (with whom Gertrude Himmelfarb begins her account of *Victorian Minds*), Tocqueville, and Acton had in this respect at least been right. Not far removed would be the suggestion that on this point, the Catholic Church in much of its social teaching, had been right. To assert that the thinking of American scholars had come to the point where this conclusion might be a logical next step, is to suggest the extent thinking had changed!

But Nisbet and his colleagues were nothing if not American in their conviction that if things are wrong they could and should be put right. Rejecting a defunct determinist tradition, he opts for outright utopianism. New institutions had to be created, or old ones revived, which, given meaningful functions, would gradually acquire authority, whereupon a multiplicity of authorities would come into existence in the interstices of which freedom would live. Citing Karl Polanyi to the effect that nineteenth century laissez-faire capitalism, which helped so to bring on the omnicompetent state, did not just happen, but was made to happen by the systematic destruction of older institutions and customs, Nisbet calls for the same process in reverse—a new laissez-faire: [7]

> To create the conditions within which autonomous *individuals* could prosper, could be emancipated from the binding ties of kinship, class, and community, was the objective of the older *laissez faire*. To create conditions within which *autonomous groups* may prosper must be . . . the prime object of the new *laissez faire*.

To revive not only Catholic social thought, but Benthamite style in social engineering is to suggest that ideology in America was changing indeed.

Nisbet had entitled one of his chapters, "History as the Decline of Community." Much that occurred in the decade of the 1950's seems to confirm that thesis. In an indirect, subtle, but probably decisive way, the experience of McCarthyism forced the left-liberal intellectuals of the country to see that the masses really were not with them on issues of fundamental importance. Slowly but emphatically the seeming all-powerful vision of the radical/liberal intellectual joined with the revolutionary/reformist mass to overthrow/humanize capitalism faded, probably never to return save in fitful alliances on behalf, not of the working class majority, but of some racial or ethnic minority. As the decade wore on, evidence of something deeply wrong in American culture seemed to accumulate. The rather low-grade if occasionally sensational forms of municipal corruption seemed to be spreading and no one seemed able to do anything about it. The problem of organized crime became serious politics: Senator Estes Kefauver in effect unseated President Truman on the issue. Trade union corruption became serious politics: John F. Kennedy made himself a national figure, and in that sense, the successor to Eisenhower on the issue. Then, towards the end of the decade the television quiz show scandals hit the country hard. Men and women who had become symbols of disinterested learning and the pursuit of excellence, and of the eventual fame that can attend such private disciplines, overnight became symbols of venality, corruption, deceit—qualities Americans may have been resigned to in politicians but emphatically assumed not to exist in the citizenry at large. In a sense, the stability of the previous arrangements had been based on the proposition that although politicians might be corrupt, the people were not, so that no very great harm could be done if the realm of politics was sufficiently restricted. Now it appeared corruption was everywhere. And indeed it might, for it would seem that of all the quiz show contenders who were given the chance to cheat, only one, an old socialist, declined.

In juvenile delinquency many of the social dangers and moral concerns of the decade came together. Whether there was in fact any more juvenile crime committed during this period than in the past is difficult to say. Probably there was not. But it did at this time assume a more threatening character, especially in New York City, which set fashions in problems no less than in clothes. Very likely the essential source of the new concern was the then forming Negro and Puerto Rican lower-class masses of the city, which had had a certain respite from proletarian violence during the 1930's and 1940's so that its reappearance seemed not an old but a new phenomenon, compounded by that special fear of black violence which Melville had grasped years earlier, and which was in time to become a near obsession of white America. But for the moment—Negro issues were still Southern issues, if issues at all—the special symbol of the new juvenile delinquency was the fighting gang. There is little reason to think this was something especially new, but it was thought to be, and for certain the Negro and Puerto Rican "boppers" did add a certain panache to the enterprise. The fighting gang was at once a threat to society and an indictment of it. (From London Richard M. Titmuss suggested that it raised for Americans the nineteenth century spectre of proletarian violence.) Too old to be helpless, but too young to be held fundamentally responsible for their acts, the delinquents called forth a special response from that element, always much in evidence in New York City, which is especially concerned with minority weaknesses when they can seem as evidence of majority failings. Government was stirred to action: new agencies and boards were added to state and city government; conferences were held; "detached workers" dispatched (an early form of direct intervention in local community processes). Sociologists and social workers came forth to do their best: more conferences were held; books by the shelfload were commissioned; some were written. Journalism did its part, as the Egyptian Kings, the Henry Street Dragons, and the Conservative Gents replaced the Hudson Dusters in the lexicon of rowdyism. In truth, imaginations *were* stirred. Avant-garde social workers began to chronicle the wars and alliances and diplomatic relations of these embattled youth with all the enthusiasm for vivid detail of nineteenth century English gentlemen historians describing the Medici. Here was life, adventure, tragedy, nobility. In a moving opera, one of the most popular musical compositions of the time, Leonard Bernstein set the tale of Romeo and Juliet amidst the fighting gangs of Manhattan's West Side.

Indeed, to a society increasingly concerned with the dessication of the community ties that lead men to accept and abide by the norms of trust, integrity, and mutual aid, the striking fact of the fighting gangs was that *they* seemed to have created for themselves genuine communities which, however pathological they might appear to the larger society, did invest the lives of the delinquents with a measure of honor, purpose, and comradeship. More than an indictment of society, more than a threat, the fighting gangs were in ways a reproach.

It is in this context, towards the end of the decade, that Paul Goodman wrote his powerful tract *Growing Up Absurd*.[8] Goodman an avowed if doctrinally elusive radical—an anarchist, if anything—was just then acquiring the great influence among middle- and upper-class college youth that was to make him in time a *guru* of the New Left in its special quest for participatory democracy. But the striking quality of his thesis in *Growing Up Absurd* is its avowed and explicitly conservative content. As with Nisbet earlier, Goodman argued the failure of so many of the liberal rationalist revolutions that had promised so much. *Democracy* had given up the ideal of true self-government and the town meeting and turned government over to a class of politicians. *The Republic* had not resulted in real political experimentation, but rather in national conformity and a "deadening centralism." *Liberty* had produced constitutional safeguards, "But with the increasing concentration of state power, and mass pressures, no effort was made to give to individuals and small groups new means easily to avail themselves of the safeguards. The result is that there is no longer the striking individuality of free men."[9] *Fraternity* had given way to a "dangerous nationalism." The *Protestant Reformation* had resulted in "secularism, individualism, the subordination of human beings to a rational economic system, and churches irrelevant to practical community life." *Syndicalism* had abandoned the ideal of worker's management in favor of higher wages that none knew how to spend well. All this, Goodman argued, "*the accumulation of the missed and compromised revolutions of modern times, with their consequent ambiguities and social imbalances, has fallen, and must fall, most heavily on the young, making it hard to grow up.*"[10] With Coleridge, he asserted that "in order to have citizens, you must first be sure that you have produced men." Men are produced by giving young people meaningful work—work that they know must be done if the community is to carry on. Goodman proposed not to turn back to earlier conceptual systems, but rather to move forward and actually finish the revolutions of liberalism. But this certainly required an outright rejection of gigantism and a reversion to smaller units of society and simpler methods of production that would connect effort and purpose. The results would look more old than new: [11]

If we are to have a stable and whole community, in which the young can grow to manhood, we must painfully perfect the revolutionary modern tradition we have. Yet this stoical resolve is, paradoxically, a *conservative* proposition, aiming at stability and social balance.

Manifestly, Goodman wrote in a radical, Jewish, intellectual tradition, addressing himself to problems of personal fulfillment. He thus faced the self-imposed difficulty of that tradition, one for recent generations at least, of demonstrating that the lower classes shared those concerns, a difficulty he resolved, however, given the prominence of juvenile delinquency as a social problem. Goodman posits a model of American society: *"an apparently closed room in which there is a large rat race as the dominant center of attention."* [12] Middle-Status Organization Men run the race, knowing it to be just that but cynically prepared to make the most of it. Working class youth "are mesmerized by the symbols and culture of the rat race" but ultimately are trapped in some factory or other, with a wife and installment payments waiting at home. Their energy level is low and their rewards meager. This is not the fate of the delinquents, a close but profoundly different group: [13]

Indeed, the group in society that most believes in the rat race as a source of value are the other underprivileged, the ignorant and resentful boys who form the delinquent gangs. In our model, we can conceive of them as running a rat race of their own, but not on the official treads.

As with the Organization Men, they are cynical, conformist, tough, one-upping, protective of their masculinity, and contemptuous of earnest slobs who do the best they can. Indeed, Goodman argues that a symbiosis of sorts has grown up between the management types and the outcasts as they exchanged styles in music, sex, clothes, and such like: "But in the alliance, the juvenile delinquents get the short end of the stick, for they esteem the rat race, though they do not get its rewards."[14]

In itself, Goodman's work is what it is: Old Testament protest. But in its time it became something more. It gave structure to a problem that had somehow escaped classification, and provided an agenda for public action. At this juncture, Norman Podhoretz, at 30, became editor of *Commentary*, the publication of the American Jewish Committee, already among the most prestigious intellectual journals of the nation and soon to enjoy a world-wide reputation. Podhoretz' first decisions as editor were being watched and he moved with what was to be accustomed boldness and brilliance. *Growing Up Absurd* had been making the rounds of publishers with no success. Podhoretz took it and, under the title, "In Search of Community," presented the main thesis as the leading article in the first issue of *Commentary* (February 1960) to appear under his editorship. He ran further excerpts in the March issue under the title, "The Calling of American Youth," and in April a final portion under the title, "Youth in the Organized Society." In his autobiography *Making It* Podhoretz states what surely is so: Goodman politicized juvenile delinquency. To argue further that the times were willing that this be done in no way detracts from the power of Goodman's rhetoric. The quest for community was acquiring momentum. It is to be noted that the formulation of the issue, and much of the momentum itself, came from the intellectual and academic world of New York where the fiercest antagonisms do not preclude but indeed are made possible by a vibrant sense of a community at work. The architect Eero Saarinen was much alive to the continuing vitality in this respect of the university world. Allan Temko writes:

> What Saarinen wished to renew, maintain, and improve was the organic expression of the *civitas* which he found weakened and virtually destroyed everywhere in modern civilizations, with one significant exception—the university campus.[15]

From these sheltered cloisters where a true understanding had been preserved, missionaries were now going forth to convert a world exhausted and ruined by technology. Indeed, for this effort a system of sorts was then being developed.

*NOTES*

1. See Daniel P. Moynihan, "The Professionalization of Reform," *The Public Interest*, Fall 1965.
2. Robert A. Nisbet, *The Quest for Community* (New York: Oxford University Press, 1953). Citations from paperback edition entitled *Community & Power* (New York: Oxford University Press, 1962).
3. *Ibid.*, pp. 3, 7.
4. *Ibid.*, p. xii.
5. *Ibid.*, pp. 49–50.
6. *Ibid.*, p. 34.
7. *Ibid.*, p. 278.
8. Paul Goodman, *Growing Up Absurd; Problems of Youth in the Organized System* (New York: Random House, 1960).
9. Paul Goodman, "In Search of Community," *Commentary*, February 1960, p. 317.
10. *Ibid.*, p. 315.
11. *Ibid.*, p. 321.

12. Paul Goodman, "The Calling of American Youth," *Commentary*, March 1960, p. 225.

13. *Ibid.*, pp. 226–27.

14. *Ibid.*, p. 227.

15. Allan Temko, *Eero Saarinen* (New York: George Braziller, 1962), p. 27. See also, Norman Podhoretz, *Making It* (New York: Random House, 1967).

# CHAPTER TWO

# THE
# PROFESSIONALIZATION
# OF
# REFORM

Thus far the origins of the community action program of the war on poverty will have appeared familiar enough. Intellectuals were doing their work—trying to make sense of the time, hoping to conceive solutions to its problems. Editors were getting it all into print; the ideas were diffusing. Now, however, a somewhat new element appears, having to do with the crucial difficulty encountered in the transition from the world of ideas to that of action. Beginning in the 1950's it becomes possible to discern the emergence of a new style—an additional style might be the more correct term—in social reform. In times past the impulse to reform and efforts in that direction had, generally speaking, risen among those groups most oppressed by existing conditions, or most likely to benefit from

21

equitable change, or from members of the public regarding middle and upper classes who, from an en-
lightened and generous understanding, were able to
identify their own interests with causes that benefited
others in the first instance but redounded ultimately to
the welfare and stability of the society as a whole.
This model—if that is not too pretentious a term—
of reform is one in which pressures for change arise
outside the institutions that are to be changed or are
capable of bringing it about. Obviously, from time to
time institutions seek to reform themselves, in the
sense that the effort arises from within. This is a matter of definition, almost, in terms of universal institutions such as the medieval Church. But in the electoral
democracies of the Atlantic world, where at any given
time only a limited number of matters are regarded as
political, the effort to bring about social change has
typically taken the form of seeking to add a particular
issue to the political agenda of the moment, thereby,
hopefully, bringing about the expenditure of public
funds or the imposition of public restraints and legal
sanctions to obtain the desired effect. Child labor, the
sale of alcohol, the chlorination of water supplies, the
beautification of highways: there was a very long list
of private concerns that were slowly translated into
public issues by persons imposing pressure on the
agencies of government—the courts, the legislature,
the executive—capable of doing what the reformers
wished done. Inasmuch as these agencies were repeatedly colonized and infiltrated by reformers there
has usually been some internal pressure in favor of
reforms, especially when the issue is quite general, as,
for example, labor legislation, and specialized government departments can be created to further the cause.
By mid-century, however, the process of external pres-

sure and internal encouragement had acquired a degree of institutionalization and expertise that might be described as the professionalization of reform. Increasingly efforts to change the American social system for the better arose from initiatives undertaken by persons whose profession was to do just that. Whereas previously the role of organized society had been largely passive—the machinery would work if someone made it work—now the process began to acquire a self-starting capacity of its own. To borrow an exaggeration from the world of automation so much in fashion at this time, the machinery began to think for itself.

This development first became evident in the Kennedy years when the national government eagerly began to seek out new ideas and programs. Kennedy's had been a severe critique of American society, whose great weakness he in effect declared was complacency, the failure to see how many things were wrong that needed righting. His election brought to Washington as officeholders, or consultants, or just friends, a striking echelon of persons whose profession might justifiably be described as knowing what ails societies and whose art is to get treatment underway before the patient is especially aware of anything noteworthy taking place.

Writing for the British journal, *The New Society*, just prior to the assassination of President Kennedy, Nathan Glazer described the process:[1]

Without benefit of anything like the Beveridge report to spark and focus public discussion and concern, the United States is passing through a stage of enormous expansion in the size and scope of what we may loosely call the social services—the public programs designed to help people adapt to an increasingly complex and unmanageable society. While Congress has been painfully and hesitantly trying to deal with two great measures—tax reform and a civil rights bill—and its deliberations on both have been closely covered by the mass media, it has also been working with much less publicity toward final passage of a number of bills which will contribute as much to changing American society.

The stalemate in American government was being broken. Already a number of major measures in the fields of regional development, mental health, vocational education, and manpower retraining had been enacted. Waiting in the wings, as Glazer put it, were a host of comparable measures whose headlong enactment in the twenty-four months or so following the assassination marked one of the most active legislative periods in the history of the Republic. But the most interesting thing about all this sudden expansion of social services was that behind it, as Glazer noted, there was "nothing like the powerful political pressure and long-sustained intellectual support that produced the great welfare measures of the New Deal—Social Security, Unemployment Insurance, Public Welfare, Public Housing."[2] Yet the programs moved forward. Lacking a better explanation, one must conclude that a new quantity had entered the equations of social change in the form of these new professionals.

It will be recalled that at this time the American poor, black and white, were surpassingly inert. The Negro civil rights movement in the South was still just that: a movement in the South for civil rights. There was almost no economic content to the protest. The American poor were not only invisible, in Michael Harrington's phrase, but they were also silent. Kennedy had ventured into West Virginia searching for Protestant votes, not for poverty. There he encountered the incredible pauperization of the mountain people, most particularly the soft-coal miners, an industrial work force whose numbers had been reduced by nearly two-thirds in the course of a decade, but with hardly a sound of protest. The miners were desperately poor, shockingly unemployed, but neither radical nor in any significant way restive. (It may be noted that in 1964, in the face of the historic Democratic sweep, Harlan County, Kentucky, returned a freshman Republican Congressman.) The Appalachian experience gave the Kennedy administration an early sensitivity to the issue of poverty and deprivation, but it was a self-imposed concern, and politically an optional one. (The decision to emphasize poverty in the 1964 legislative program, which would set the theme for the presidential year, was a close one: a strong case was made within the administration to address the 1964 campaign to problems of the suburbs, where many of the trade union members in the nation had settled.) The war on poverty was not declared at the behest of the poor: it was declared in their interest by persons confident of their own judgment in such matters. As Glazer put it, at a time when the process was not at all as visible as it was to become,[3] the fate of poor:

Is in the hands of the administrators and the professional organizations of doctors, teachers, social workers, therapists, counselors, and so forth. It is these who, in a situation where the legislation and programs become ever more complex, spend the time to find out—or rather have brought home to them through their work—the effects of certain kinds of measures and programs, and who propose ever more complex programs which Congress deliberates upon in the absence of any major public interest. When Congress argues these programs, the chief pressures are not the people, but the organized professional interests that work with that segment of the problem, and those who will benefit from or be hurt by the legislation.

Four major influences can be perceived behind this development.

1. *The econometric revolution.* Although it is still too soon to speak with full confidence, the likelihood grows that in the area of economic policy there was a

genuine discontinuity associated with World War II: before it men did not know how to make an industrial economy work at high and expanding levels of activity; afterwards they did. The combination of Keynesian theory and the increasingly sophisticated and dependable quantification of economic movements, associated with such men as Wesley C. Mitchell and Simon Kuznets provided for the first time a working model of an industrial economy that permitted a very high order of successful management. That such success would be greatest in a society with no politics, and that in certain conditions of political deadlock or disorder the best model imaginable is of no practical use, need not detract from the fact that the political leaders of the 1960's in the United States *were* able to make use of this new knowledge. In the other industrial democracies of the world, or such as were left of them, memories of the political disasters that accompanied the prolonged economic depressions of the 1920's and 1930's had provided the strongest of incentives to maintain high levels of employment. (In 1964, unemployment, adjusted to conform more or less to United States definitions, was 2.9 per cent in Italy, 2.5 per cent in France and Britain, and 0.4 per cent in Germany. Consider the contrast with the unemployment that followed the First World War.) Postwar America had experienced a not less extraordinary economic growth, albeit erratic and associated with much more joblessness. Under Kennedy, however, an immensely powerful and competent political economy took hold. Growth became steady, unemployment declined, the future became predictable in a way it had never been. (The Council of Economic Advisors' forecast of Gross National Product for 1964 was off by only $400 million in a total of $623 billion, while the unemployment forecast was on the nose.) In an unbroken expansion, the longest in American economic history, the GNP grew from $503.7 billion in 1960 to $807.6 in the last quarter of 1967, with an implicit price deflator, using 1958 dollars, at the end of the period of only 118.9. What the future might hold remained as uncertain as ever, but it did become clear in this period that the American economy was moving ahead powerfully, and properly managed, could continue to do so.

The foreseeable results of this transformation were many, of which two were notable in the context of the professionalization of reform. The first is that if the economy were to continue to expand, the number of persons in economic difficulties would contract, or at least not grow. Already a minority, the poor would certainly remain one, and very likely become even more so. There would be less and less reason then to expect mass political support for social reform, at least to the extent that such support in the past had reflected the immediate, individual interests of an electoral majority. The principal sources of political power in a capitalist democracy being votes and money, and the poor having an insufficiency of either, it was more or less ordained that they should become in some degree clients of persons interested in their plight and professionally competent in terms of knowledge of the subject and access to power. This relationship is perhaps never more evident than when the professional reformer encourages the client to insist that only the "indigenous disadvantaged" can truly understand their problems and accordingly they should be given the power to make decisions about it.

A further and not less decisive result of the econometric revolution was the quite startling reversal of the position of the money managers of the executive branch of the Federal government. The conservative

press to the contrary, the expenditure programs of the
Federal government are managed on principles, or
strategies, not different from those of most large organizations. The normal presumption, and the normal
condition, is that resources are scarce and that the
demand for them will outrun the supply. In consequence allocation is turned over to specialists, in the
case of the Federal government to the Bureau of
the Budget, the Council of Economic Advisors, and the
Treasury, whose task, as much as anything, is to say
"no." Big decisions are sorted out and reserved for the
President and his staff, but typically these are matters
where the necessity to prefer one set of allocations
over another has such political significance as to preclude a surrogate decision by the permanent civil service. Under conditions of high and steady economic
expansion, however, a quite extraordinary reversal of
this process takes place. Expenditures under existing
Federal programs rise at a fairly predictable rate. But
revenues from the existing tax structure rise even
faster. Of a sudden—by mid-decade this was clearly
discernible in Washington—the immediate *supply* of
resources bids fair to outrun the *demand* for them.
Thus in the summer of 1965 the President's advisors
publicly estimated that Federal revenues would increase by some $35 billion by 1970, starting at an
annual increment of $4–5 billion and rising to about
$7 billion. Without great exaggeration, it could be said
that social policy during that period would be determined by the way in which the $35 billion was allo-
cated. (Alas, almost immediately it was allocated to
the war in Vietnam, but that is another tale.) The
crucial point is that under the theory of fiscal management that evolved during this time, there was *no*
option but to expend the surplus. The concept of "fiscal
drag" held that unless the revenue increment of the

Federal fisc is immediately returned to the economy it begins to have a depressing effect. This, in a word, was money you had to spend in order to get. The result was the beginning of a situation utterly without parallel in modern government: administrations that must be constantly on the lookout for new ways to expend public funds in the public interest. (In addition to various forms of tax reduction.) This is precisely the type of decision-making that is suited to the techniques of modern organization, and that ends up in the hands of persons who make a profession of it. A side effect: as such decisions become more professional, they are likely to become less political, in the sense of responding to existing power configurations.

2] *The exponential growth of knowledge.* The econometric revolution was not an isolated event: precisely to the contrary, it was part of the extraordinary growth in knowledge of the twentieth century, with all its accompanying forms of instability. The economy may yet suffer utter collapse, just as we may yet blow ourselves up: intermediary miscalculations are not only to be seen as possible, but to be expected. But the master term is that of miscalculation: fewer and fewer basic decisions in the society are made without some form of quantified knowledge being brought to bear on them. It can be said of the war on poverty that it began not because it was necessary, but because it was possible. The funds were available, not only *despite* the tax reduction of 1964, but in measure *because* of it. But this was not the only sense in which it had become possible. The same quantified knowledge of the economy which was making economic theory increasingly operational was also pointing up social problems that persisted despite the onset of persistent prosperity. In the aftermath of World War II the proposition gained favor that whereas the early stages of capitalism led to an accentuation of income inequality, the later stages reversed this trend, so that the extremes grew closer, and there was much clustering at the median. During the 1950's, however, the researches of Robert J. Lampman began to challenge this hypothesis. (Apparently a process of equalization had been going on during the war, to be reversed during the Republican years that followed. This is precisely what occurred during and after World War I.) Never without influence in Washington (his original work was widely disseminated by the Joint Committee on the Economic Report), Lampman was especially close to the economists who took office with Kennedy, and his demonstration of persisting and even worsening income maldistribution provided a powerful, and early influence on the administration to move in this direction.

But this is but one instance. Among the complexities of American life is that the American business community, during the first half of the twentieth century when it was fiercely opposed to the idea of economic or social planning, nonetheless supported, even pressed for, the development of a national statistical system that largely as a result of this support became perhaps the best in the world. This in turn made certain types of planning and regulation feasible, and in a measure, inevitable. John Kenneth Galbraith has noted the indispensable role of statisticians in modern societies, which seem never to do anything about problems until they learn to measure them, that being the special province of those applied mathematicians. Statistics are used as mountains are climbed: because they are there. If one recalls that the nation went through the entire depression of the 1930's without ever really knowing what the unemployment rate was (the statistic was then gathered once each ten years by the

Census Bureau), one gains a feeling for the great expansion of knowledge in this and related fields in the quarter century that followed. By the 1960's, the monthly employment data had become a vital, sensitive, and increasingly reliable source of information about American society, and that information increasingly insisted that although the majority of Americans were prosperous indeed, a significant minority were not.

The success of the economists in mastering the problems they set themselves has been in some measure at least a reflection of investment in the field. If the natural sciences have been by far the more robust and productive, it must be noted that they have received the greater proportion of manpower and research funds. As of 1964, two-thirds of the Ph.D.'s in the United States were in the natural sciences, more than a quarter in chemistry alone. The social sciences had but 7 per cent of all Ph.D.'s, with economists outnumbering sociologists five to one. Even so, the social sciences were experiencing a roughly proportional expansion in research support. In 1964, overall expenditure for social science research was somewhere between $500 and $600 million, a tenth of the $6 billion spent that year on the life and physical sciences, including psychology. In 1956, the Federal government had obligated a mere $4 million to social science research. By 1966, this had risen to $44 million, and reached an estimated $59 million for 1968. At such rates of expenditure it is to be expected that there would be some increase in knowledge, and almost certainly during this period there was. Nothing especially dramatic, and tending to be more descriptive than otherwise; nonetheless, it is a fact that as the resources available for social reform were increasing, so were the sources of information by which such reforms might be guided.

31

3. *The professionalization of the middle class.*
"Everywhere in American life," Kenneth S. Lynn reports, "the professions are triumphant."[4] The period since the G. I. Bill has witnessed an extraordinary expansion of higher education. In the United States, a quarter of the teenage population now goes on to some kind of college, and among specific class and ethnic groups, the proportion is as high as three-quarters. The trend is unmistakable and probably irresistible; in the course of the coming decades some form of education beyond high school will become near to universal. But most importantly, for more and more persons the form of education will involve professional training. This is something different from mere higher education; it produces a different type of person.

That difference has been most succinctly stated by Everett C. Hughes: "Professionals *profess*. They profess to know better than others the nature of certain matters, and to know better than their clients what ails them or their affairs." And he continues:[5]

Lawyers not only give advice to clients and plead their cases for them; they also develop a philosophy of law—of its nature and its functions, and of the proper way in which to administer justice. Physicians consider it their prerogative to define the nature of disease and of health, and to determine how medical services ought to be distributed and paid for. Social workers are not content to develop a technique of case work; they concern themselves with social legislation. Every profession considers itself the proper body to set the terms in which some aspect of society, life or nature is to be thought of, and to define the general lines, or even the details, of public policy concerning it.

This development is in a sense only one aspect of the general triumph of the graduate school, of which David Riesman and Christopher Jencks have written. Professors produce professionals. (In itself this is rather a new process; in the not far distant past apprenticeship was the common mode of access to many such callings.) And as the number of professionals has increased, so has the number of professions. More and more, middle-class persons are attracted to the independence of judgment, esoteric knowledge, and relative immunity to outside criticism that characterize professional occupations. Professional prerogatives are increasingly asserted in previously rather mundane fields. Again, Everett Hughes: "The YMCA secretary wants his occupation recognized not merely as that of offering young men from the country a pleasant road to Protestant righteousness in the city, but as a more universal one dealing with groups of young people. All that is learned of adolescence, of behavior in small groups, of the nature and organization of community life is considered the intellectual base of his work."[6]

There are now an extraordinary number of such professionals in America. The National Science Foundation estimates that the number of scientists and engineers alone *nearly doubled* between 1950 and 1965, a rate of growth 4.5 times that of the labor force as a whole. At mid-decade, the number of persons classified as professional and technical workers passed the nine million mark—a number greater than that of managers, officials, and proprietors, greater even than the number of craftsmen and foremen. And of this group, a considerable number are involved in various aspects of social welfare and reform. Through sheer numbers they would tend to have their way; but as professionals in a professionalizing society, they are increasingly entitled to have their way. That is how the system works. As has been said, the war on poverty resulted in the first instance from a variety of professional judgments concerning the persistence of the problem and the need for certain levels of Federal expenditure. Inevitably the content of the effort and the kind of program that resulted was similarly influenced by professional judgments. Whatever exactly is meant by the term "the poor," it will be clear enough that they had almost nothing whatever to do with the process.

4. *The rise of the foundations.* Philanthropy has been a characteristic feature of American society almost from its inception. Although it began and continues to be associated with voluntary contributions of relatively small sums to religious organizations, these contributions have been in no small measure destined for social welfare purposes, and as the society has grown more secularized, so has social welfare philanthropy. In the settlement house movement of the turn of the century, philanthropy took an activist role, associating itself not only with the cause of the poor, but also directly involving itself with the life of poor communities. With the rise of the foundations, however, a fundamental change took place. There came into being a number of organizations with immense and (within the limits of common law prohibitions) permanent financial resources, which by and large identified themselves with the advancement of knowledge and with liberal social change. The process was at first slow enough. The Carnegie Corporation and the various Rockefeller funds dominated the foundation scene and were fairly cautious. Gradually, however, a number of smaller foundations were established, many reflecting the more pronouncedly liberal traditions of Jewish politics and philosophy, which took much more adventurous and interventionist roles, especially in areas of Negro needs. The Stern Family Fund, the Field Foundation, the New World Foundation, the J. M. Kaplan Fund, the Taconic Foundation, are names that come readily to mind. But the decisive event came in 1950 when the Ford Foundation, established in 1936 "to serve the public welfare through grants

for educational, scientific, and charitable purposes," largely local in nature, received a tremendous grant from the Ford family and became, in its words, "a nationwide philanthropy." Immediately Ford, with resources that in time rose above three billion dollars dominated the foundation world. In the period 1950–63, upwards of $1.9 billion in grants were made, 90 per cent to institutions within the United States, primarily colleges, universities, schools, and community organizations. This latter category represents a major innovation; it had major consequences for American society.

With the advent of Ford, the professional style in reform plunged forward. From the outset, Ford took the initiative in deciding what needed to be done. A Public Affairs Program was established as one of the nine grant-making programs of the foundation. Paul N. Ylvisaker, an energetic, creative social innovator came to head it. (The sheer size of the foundation apparently gave immense powers to the professional "philanthropoids," in Dwight MacDonald's phrase, who were employed by the foundation. It is reasonable to assume that on balance these were far more politically liberal than the trustees. Rather as television took editorializing away from Republican publishers and turned it over to Democratic reporters, the huge contemporary foundation has done something of the same to what once was termed charity.) From the outset, the Public Affairs Program adopted the urban theme as its motif. Speaking in 1963, Ylvisaker stated, "Hardly a grant among the $100 million we have committed over the past decade does not in one way or another address itself to urban problems and conditions."[7]

At first grants tended to emphasize research and study, but gradually these gave way to programs of direct action, the so-called "grey areas" program. A number of deteriorating central city areas were chosen, and foundation funds made avaliable not just to help with ongoing work or to provide needed services that were not available, but rather to transform the political and social life of the community through new community organization. Ylvisaker described the effort in terms of three "tough and diverse jobs": [8]

—of trying to mesh the policies and operations of separate public and private jurisdictions;
—of working with disadvantaged and minority groups, particularly the Negro community;
—of looking beyond old and fixed ways of doing things, to invent and evaluate new approaches in education, housing, employment, legal services, and welfare.

The object, Ylvisaker boldly stated, was "to experiment with new ways of improving the social conditions of the central city and of opening new opportunities to those now living in these urban 'grey areas.'" Whereupon he claimed for the effort the distinguishing quality of the professional style in reform: the ability to anticipate problems, and to know best: [9]

These grants were conceived and negotiated before the current wave of civil-rights protest began. They were not and are not intended as substitutes for protest, which has always been a healthy part of American politics and community improvement. Rather, they are intended to help correct the basic conditions which have led to protest, and to develop the latent potential of the human beings now crowded and often crushed at the bottom of the community's totem pole.

Thus community action became one of the first major themes in this new style in social change.

*NOTES*

1. Nathan Glazer, "A New Look in Social Welfare" in *New Society*, 7 November 1963, p. 6.

2. *Ibid.*

3. *Ibid.*

4. Kenneth S. Lynn: "Introduction to the Issue 'The Professions' " in *Daedalus*, Vol. 92 No. 4, Fall 1963, p. 649.

5. Everett C. Hughes, "Professions" in *Daedalus*, Vol. 92, No. 4, Fall 1963, pp 656–7.

6. *Ibid.*

7. Paul N. Ylvisaker, "A Foundation Approach to City Problems," in *American Community Development*, Preliminary Reports by Directors of Projects Assisted by the Ford Foundation in Four Cities and a State, p. 5.

8. *Ibid.*, p. 8.

9. *Ibid.*, pp. 6–7.

# CHAPTER THREE

# MOBILIZATION
# FOR
# YOUTH

The grey areas program of the Ford Foundation is to be understood not only in terms of the intellectual ferment of the period, but also of the political listlessness. It originated, as Marris and Rein observe, "at a time when a divided Congress under a conservative president was neither willing nor able to initiate major reforms. The projects had therefore been conceived primarily in terms of a power vacuum: by concerting a coherent leadership in cities, they hoped to demonstrate how reform might circumvent the stultification of national policy."[1] Ylvisaker diagnosed two fundamental problems of these urban grey areas. First, that of a cycle of poverty in which the, for the most part, newly migrated population was caught up and from which it could not escape without a considerable measure of social intervention. Second, a rigidification of bureaucratic processes within those institutions nominally responsible for such social intervention—schools, welfare agencies, employment offices, and so on—so that in fact their interventions did not succeed and the poverty cycle continued. If Ylvisaker brought all the expertise and manner of a reform professional to his enterprises, he is also to be seen as a deeply religious man, striving for understanding and reconciliation. Marris and Rein describe his carefully prepared and widely distributed speeches during this period:[2]

He argued . . . for a programme of reform which would at once respect the diversity and individualism of city life, and release it from its collective impotence. His speeches search after the political alchemy that would transmute the institutionalized expression of a common purpose into ungoverned personal action. "What is needed to co-ordinate and exploit the inherent power of the complicated, egalitarian societies is the development in balance of far more sophisticated nervous, circulatory and other systems than have been evolved either by our nation or any other. To detect and anticipate; to correlate and differentiate; to probe and carry through; to mobilize and individualize; to gather power and liberate it." The agencies of reform were therefore to act as facilitators, analysts and catalysers, crystallizing the good intentions of many people about a common endeavour, yet without imposing on their freedom.

The assumption of common good intentions was both natural to Ylvisaker and necessary to his work. On what other grounds could a private, tax-free foundation, representing a major capitalist interest, use its money to reorder the politics of the poor? This is fundamental. Marris and Rein continue:[3]

Taken together, the conceptions of a poverty cycle and of bureaucratic introversion explained the breakdown of assimilation to the opportunity structure without presupposing any fundamental conflict of interest. On both sides, the breakdown was seen in terms of irrational self-frustration.

Even so, he had to be careful. Hence the efforts of the Ford Foundation at this time were ostensibly directed exclusively to the somehow apolitical question of *process*. Ylvisaker had no *program* for social reform, only a *method* whereby local communities could evolve their own. Without the intervention of the outside agency nothing was going to happen, but that intervention assumed a form that protected it against the charge of interference. Local participation ensured the legitimacy of the results, a formula frequently to be encountered in the years that followed. The name of the game was community action, the vehicle that of the independent community agency.

In an address given in January 1963 entitled, "Community Action: A Response to Some Unfinished Business," Ylvisaker presents a useful outline of the thinking of the Ford Foundation on this subject at that time. He describes, first of all, his technique. The problems cities faced were enormous: "migration, automation, racial tensions, relaxing moral standards, exploding populations, accelerating technological progress and obsolescence." An impressive list, in which it may be noted that "progress," too, had become a problem. To deal with them, Ylvisaker proposed, the "social application of the art of jujitsu: of exerting smaller forces at points of maximum leverage to capture larger forces otherwise working against us." (A compelling image, but not an entirely clear one: just what is to be thrown off balance?) He then described four "hunches" with which the Foundation had proceeded. First, that the city could be conceived of as a system, "much as A.T. & T., for example, has long viewed it as a communication system." Systems analysts should be put to work "on the social production system of the modern metropolis." (This became, of course, the avowed purpose of the Urban Institute established by the Johnson Administration in 1968, with the help of Ford Foundation funds: a kind of jujitsu.) The second hunch was that "*awakening self-respect is the most powerful agent for renewing our cities socially, and for that matter physically.*" The third hunch was that "certain parts of the urban social system can be perfected by rational means and specific devices." Contrasting with the urban renewal program of the 1940's, he continued:

We have placed the Ford Foundation's first bet not on the central business district of the city but on its school system, and more on school outlook and methods than on buildings; on the city and metropolitan area's employment system, on their administration of justice, and a growing list of similarly critical "production processes" which are currently bottlenecks in the process of citizen-building.

His final hunch was that "it would be a mistake to assume that ingenious social inventions could not arise from agencies which already existed in the community." There is an element of ingenuousness here, much as in the remark of the Earl of Kildare's that he would not have burned a church had he not thought the Bishop was in it. The Ford Foundation did not begin with the assumption that ingenious social invention could not arise from existing community agencies, but somehow it always ended with that conclusion. Indeed by this time the Foundation had already reached that conclusion with respect to four cities and provided funds to establish new community agencies in Boston, New Haven, Oakland, and Philadelphia.

In the aftermath of the enactment of the poverty program, and of related enterprises such as the Model Cities Program, the establishment of new community organizations, with ever more ingenious acronymic flourishes, has become commonplace. This was not so at the beginning of the 1960's. The use of Federal funds for such efforts was unheard of; such New Deal experiments that had occurred had been discredited if they had failed, and forgotten if they had not. Community Chest types of organizations, which began in the 1920's and spread throughout the nation, were essentially fund-raising devices designed to provide an orderly system of support for private, nonprofit social service agencies, typically providing family services. The Ford Foundation had something far more enterprising in mind: it purposed nothing less than institutional change in the operation and control of American cities. To this object it came forth with a social invention of enormous power: the independent community agency. In effect, the Public Affairs Program of the Ford Foundation invented a new level of American government, the inner-city community action agency.

The idea that a private, tax-free organization, responsible to none but its own wishes, should attempt anything of the sort would surely have given rise to not a little consternation in liberal circles had the organization been seen as politically conservative. But the intentions of the Foundation were so impeccably benign that the subject was hardly raised, if at all. Moreover, the need for such efforts, the conviction of the decline of community and the alienation of the urban mass was almost a "given." The usefulness of an independent community agency, designed to involve local persons in the control of their own destinies needed hardly to be argued among persons who followed such matters. The contrast between the shaggy, inexact communitarian anarchism of the Paul Goodman variety, which characterized this aspect of the Ford Foundation program, with the shiny, no nonsense, city-as-a-system, Robert S. McNamara style of the other part, need not distract anyone. At the time, those ostensibly divergent tendencies seemed somehow equally up-to-date and mutually compatible. Again, the times seemed to facilitate such convergence, as was to be seen in Nisbet's call for a system of institutional laissez-faire, or in a not dissimilar observation of Marris and Rein:[4]

[L]iberal reform, like the radical right, seems to be appealing to a tradition of individualism which bureaucracy has corrupted. But unlike the right, it recognizes the justice of institutional intervention, from generation to generation, to restore an equal chance, and seeks to make that intervention more effective.

In truth, the Ford Foundation was not the first to conceive of an umbrella type of community agency with objectives of this kind. The prototype began on the Lower East Side of New York—a traditional, almost a classical area of immigrant settlement in the great city, which, following World War II, had begun to fill up with the most recent newcomers, Puerto Ricans and Southern Negroes. With them had come the old problem of juvenile delinquency; the "fighting gangs" of the period, with their exotic names and systematized violence, half Renaissance, half Iroquois, and the appearance of drug use as a distinctly lower class, youthful phenomenon. In the context of the current theories of alienation and the decline of community, seemed to call for a special response. At a meeting of the Board of Directors of the Henry Street Settlement, in June 1957, the businessman-philanthropist J. M. Kaplan proposed "that work be started at once on drawing up a program commensurate in size and scope with the dimensions of the problem." What came to be known as Mobilization for Youth was thereupon officially begun.

Neither the size of the area nor the scope of the problem was overwhelming, which was just as well if something importantly new was to be tried. The territory consisted of five health areas, as defined by the

New York City Department of Health, comprising altogether thirteen census tracts. Just over 100,000 persons lived there, in the city of eight million. (It may be noted that 1960 population was barely one-third that of 1910, when the Henry Street Settlement was earning its deserved reputation in a teeming slum of 299,459 persons. Thus do standards of deprivation change.) It was not an especially unruly neighborhood; the juvenile delinquency rate there had been consistently lower than that of Manhattan as a whole, although greater than the city as a whole. The reason for this was simple enough. The largest ethnic group in the area continued to be Jewish, and as the organization's prospectus observed, "Only one Jewish boy was reported as currently in a gang." Jewish and Italian boys (another sizable group) at this stage in New York history were not getting into trouble, certainly not in the proportion of Negro and Puerto Rican youth, ethnic groups that made up 8 per cent and 26 per cent of the area population respectively. Other, more troubled neighborhoods could have been found, but the Henry Street Settlement was where it was and that is where the action occurred.

In short order, Mobilization for Youth, Inc. (MFY) was founded as a "non-profit membership corporation composed of representatives of agencies and institutions on the Lower East Side of New York City and persons recommended by the New York School of Social Work at Columbia University." A Board of Directors was assembled, headed by the impeccably patrician Winslow Carlton. He was joined by the familiar assemblage: a priest, a rabbi, a minister, a Negro, a Puerto Rican, a trade unionist, a woman. The principal settlement houses in the area were represented. Notably, both the Dean of the New York School of Social Work of Columbia University, P. Frederick DelliQuadri, and the Associate Dean, Mitchell I. Ginsberg, were members. The Board very much represented the welfare establishment in the era of Robert F. Wagner and had ready access to City Hall. Funds were provided by the Kaplan Foundation to set in motion a planning process that was to go on for four and one-half years, with additional support in time from the Taconic Foundation, headed by the late Stephen Currier, the National Institute of Mental Health, and most importantly, the New York School of Social Work.

The Lower East Side of New York, if it no longer teemed with slum dwellers, had more than its share of social agencies, a legacy from the swarming immigrant past. These agencies had at least the normal capacity to devise "action programs" to justify their existence, and in truth with the arrival of the Negro and Puerto Rican groups, they had every reason to wish to do so. But much of the conviction had drained out of the old ways of social work. Perhaps also in subtle ways it was perceived or suspected that those old ways, whatever their validity might once have been, would not be as effective with the new clients, as social workers prefer to call those whose dependence on them is often as painful for the middle-class professional as it is for the lower class recipient. A new approach seemed called for, one that would respond not only to the possibly different needs of Negroes and Puerto Ricans and also —this surely was an influence—to the general sense of the attrition of the urban community, and the emerging social science doctrines as to the sources of this attrition. In a paper prepared for a Ford Foundation Conference Discussion on Community Development held in October 1960, Lloyd E. Ohlin of Columbia's School of Social Work set forth the proposition that in such efforts one of the central issues is, "What are the conditions of life in deprived urban

45

areas which should be viewed as problematic."[5] MFY chose juvenile delinquency, and this was decisive, as a theory of social action to combat delinquency had by then emerged which brought together the essential themes of alienation, community, moral values, and social change. This was the "opportunity" theory of delinquent behavior propounded in the book *Delinquency and Opportunity*, published that year by Ohlin and his colleague at the Columbia School of Social Work, Richard A. Cloward.[6]

Before describing the Cloward-Ohlin thesis, it would be well to suggest the essential sterility of official approaches to the problem of delinquency at this time. Much that followed will be forgiven if the reader considers what went before.

A fair representation will be found in the *Report to Congress on Juvenile Delinquency*, prepared and submitted by the Children's Bureau and the National Institute of Mental Health, agencies of the Department of Health, Education and Welfare, in 1960. The work was largely that of the Children's Bureau, established a half century earlier in the era of child labor. With that problem long since supplanted by the issue of youth unemployment, the Children's Bureau kept busy by finding new problems. In 1954, a Division of Juvenile Delinquency Service was established and in time it produced the inevitable report to Congress.

Delinquency posed for the Children's Bureau the same form of dilemma that family instability in Negroes was later to present: an issue fascinating as it might justify the Bureau's existence, but terrifying as it raised questions of immoral behavior. The Bureau's strategy on both issues was to say nothing itself but to attack the position of anyone who did. The position of the 1960 report to Congress, largely the work of the Children's Bureau, is summed up in one paragraph.

Many factors frequently cited as causes of delinquency are really only concomitants. They are not causes in the sense that if they were removed delinquency would decline. Among these factors are:

Broken homes.
Poverty.
Poor housing.
Lack of recreational facilities.
Poor physical health.
Race.
Working mothers.[7]

Travis Hirschi and Hanan C. Selvin, in an article devoted to the report, have termed this the thesis that "nothing causes anything."[8] The report abounds in ponderous findings:

Juvenile delinquency is a total national problem that is increasing both in absolute and relative terms.

Delinquency is still most prevalent among lower social economic groups and in deteriorated sections of large cities, but it occurs also in more favored parts of cities and communities. The rate of increase in delinquency in rural areas and small towns appears to be even more rapid, in recent years, than in large urban centers.

The factors related to the occurrence of juvenile delinquency are so numberous and complex that only extremely well-coordinated approaches utilizing all of the governmental and nongovernmental resources of our society—local, state, and national—can hope to be effective in curbing the present trend.

The prediction of delinquency in children and the techniques of prevention are not well understood.

Today, services for both the prevention of delinquency and the treatment and rehabilitation of offenders are inadequate for reasons of lack of coordination. . . .

There is also a great need for strengthening at all levels the organization, coordination, and staffing of agencies both public and private.

It concluded that the Federal government should play a "leadership" role—a Washington term meaning genuine responsibility would remain elsewhere—but also specifically recommended that research and demonstration projects "in different types and sizes of communities, among varying groups in the population, and in different kinds of programs designed for prevention, control, and treatment of juvenile delinquency" should be undertaken. Special stress was laid on the evaluation of such programs. The routine proposal for dealing in some unspecified way with the "acute shortage of adequately trained personnel" constituted the second of the report's two recommendations.

In effect the report was a summary of research findings of the period which demonstrated that no single factor yet tested bore a *perfect* relationship to delinquency. Fair enough. The great value of such findings, as A. K. Cohen has stated, is that they invalidate "the assumption of intrinsic pathogenic qualities" of "broken homes," or "poor housing," or "race," or whatever. But to go from there to assume that what has no *intrinsic* pathogenic qualities, has no pathogenic qualities whatever is both fatal in logic and stultifying in action. Hirschi and Selvin write:[9]

[P]erfect association implies single causation, and less-than-perfect association implies multiple causation. Rejecting as causes of delinquency those variables whose association is less than perfect thus implies rejecting the principle of multiple causation. * * * Rejecting the principle of multiple causation implies denying the possibility of *any* change in the social structure—since, in this view, nothing causes anything.

This was emphatically not the view of Cloward and Ohlin, who found in alienation the master concept for explaining and controlling delinquency. In this they were following an already well-established tradition. As Nisbet observed, just as twentieth century artists, writers, theologians, and political philosophers became preoccupied with the plight of the isolated individual in his unequal contest with a Protestant God or capitalist state, "So too in the social sciences has the vision of the lost individual become central."[10] This began with the French sociologist Émile Durkheim who, at the turn of the century investigated the phenomenon of suicide and found it closely related to a sense of normlessness, an absence or dissication of moral and social involvement with others, which he termed *anomie*. The correlates of the anomic variant alienation were familiar features of the twentieth century: the more urbanized, rationalized, industrialized, unaffiliated the individual, the more likely he would lose faith in others, give in to despair—one of the seven deadly sins of the old faith—and turn to self destruction.

Melvin Seeman has isolated, as it were, five related but distinguishable notions of alienation that can be defined in terms of an individual's expectancies and values. These are: *powerlessness, meaninglessness, normlessness, value isolation,* and *self-estrangement*. Seeman contrasts these with the positive values that go into the making of a stable and rewarding society:[11]

The sense of powerlessness goes counter to the values of *mastery and autonomy;* value isolation undercuts the goal of *consensus;* normlessness threatens the stable development of *order and trust;* while meaninglessness and self estrangement are the alienative counterparts of *understanding and commitment.*

Social scientists have had some success in scaling such attitudes and in measuring the correlations between them. Notably stable scaling has been achieved for the concepts of powerlessness and of anomie. The two correlate, but they are not the same. In general, the lower an individual is in the socioeconomic hierarchy, the higher will be his scores on these attitudes. *But anomie does appear to identify social deviant persons, whereas powerlessness does not.*[12]

This association became one of central interest to

the eminent Columbia sociologist Robert K. Merton (coeditor with Nisbet of the study *Contemporary Social Problems*[13]) who, writing in the mid-1950's, held that anomie arises when there is a disjunction between socially approved goals and social institutions through which such goals must be achieved. The consequence is deviant behavior. Norms result from interaction between cultural values, social structures, and individual needs. When the structures do not permit the needs to be fulfilled within the guidelines of the cultural values, the latter begin to lose their meaning, certainly their authority.[14] Merton in a sense worked *back* from findings concerning individuals to conclusions concerning the society, this in the tradition of Harry Stack Sullivan who insisted that personal disorders are often but reflections of social disorders. In an incisive and persuasive next step, Cloward and Ohlin took this set of concepts to explain the behavior, or misbehavior, of the Henry Street Dragons. Delinquency, they argued, arises when socially approved goals—owning a car, dressing well—are made impossible to achieve through legitimate methods, because of motor vehicle licensing requirements, lack of part-time jobs for juveniles, and so on. The delinquent is a normal youth with normal expectations that society does not permit him to achieve through normal channels. Whereupon he turns to alternate channels, which typically are illegal. Lacking opportunity to earn money to buy clothes, he steals it. His willingness to do this is not callousness but normlessness, an anomic condition induced by society.

There is nothing uniquely American about anomie. To the contrary, it is a common phenomenon of modern industrial societies. (Belmondo's unthinking murderer in "Breathless" is normless, as it is Jean Seberg, who turns him in.) It will also be seen, however, that the thesis as related to delinquency was reassuringly conservative, quintessentially American. A half century of international sociology had produced a set of propositions not far from Father Flanagan's assertion that "There is no such thing as a bad boy." Cloward and Ohlin argued that delinquents were resorting to desperately deviant and dangerous measures in order to *conform* to the routine goals of the larger society. If that society wished them to conform not only in their objectives but in their means for achieving them, it had only to provide the *opportunity* to do so. Opportunity was the master concept. And what else was America all about? But this was precisely where so much advanced social thinking of that time was emerging. What, after all, had Paul Goodman, radical, bohemian, leftist theorist, asked of society save that young men be given meaningful work to do?

The planning for MFY proceeded for four and one-half years, a time span which will give some feeling of the professional care and hopefully scientific attitude that went into its preparation. At length, on December 9, 1961, the results were published in a 617-page volume entitled *A Proposal for the Prevention and Control of Delinquency by Expanding Opportunities*.[15] This was, in effect, a request for the National Institute of Mental Health to fund the project. The volume is one of the more remarkable documents in the history of efforts to bring about "scientific" social change: lucid, informed, precise, scholarly, and above all, candid. A plan devised by a group of middle-class intellectuals to bring about changes in the behavior of a group of lower class youth who differed from them in ethnicity and religion, in social class and attitudes, in life styles, and above all, in life prospects. An enterprise, designed in the most avowed and open manner, to acquire by the experimental mode knowledge of general validity that could be applied elsewhere with predictable results. As the Prospectus states: [16]

> Juvenile delinquency is widely recognized as a major social problem not only in the United States but in many other modern industrial countries throughout the world. Yet little systematic work has been done on the problem since the Second World War. Law enforcement officers and the courts, social welfare, religious and civic organizations, and government at various levels, all have taken a crack at it but only on a fragmentary, ad hoc basis. While behavioral scientists have formulated a number of theories of causation and process, their hypotheses have gone largely untested.
>
> "Mobilization for Youth" is put forward as an answer to the need for a systematic approach to the problem. . . . It offers a broad program of action based on a coherent operating hypothesis and integrated with a carefully designed program of research and evaluation. Essentially, it is a project of social experimentation and investigation, using as its laboratory an urban residential area with a high delinquency rate, large and diverse enough in population to be representative of problem areas in many communities but small enough geographically to permit the operation of intensive programs of action and research.

The analogy with laboratory research in the physical sciences was not simply a manner of speaking; it was the specific and avowed intent of the project to produce valid and replicable results that could then be used generally. The Prospectus continued: [17]

> It is a large and expensive project as behavioral science experiments go, but compared with projects in technological research and development it is modest. We think that it is time that American society began to invest something like as much in the development of better human relations as it puts into technology. As in industry and the physical sciences, social research and development costs far more than the subsequent application of its findings and the replication of the methods it tests.

After a brief depiction of conditions in the MFY Area, the Prospectus moves directly to a detailed account of the theoretical foundations on which the proposed program was to be based. Cloward and Ohlin's theory was represented as "an effort to extend and to refine two great intellectual traditions: the theory of anomie, as exemplified in the work of Émile Durkheim and Robert K. Merton, and the theory of culture transmission and differential association, as exemplified in the work of Clifford R. Shaw, Henry D. McKay and Edwin H. Sutherland."[18] Theretofore theories of delinquency had tended to locate the problem within the delinquent individual, howsoever much society may be responsible for his having ended up in such a condition. One theory, that of culture conflict, suggested that lower-class youth "internalize" a value system from their milieu which leads—in some ways, requires —them to behave in a manner that the larger middle-class society defines as delinquent. The youth do nothing particularly wrong by the lights of their immediate society, but such actions are deemed delinquent by the larger society. Another theory described delinquency as a kind of *rite de passage* in which the gang provides a setting in which a youth passing into manhood can perform the prescribed feats of testing and daring. Yet another, and related one, saw delinquency as especially associated with the female-based households so common to lower-class life which provide adolescent males no models by which to ease out of the childhood identification with mother, with the result that they have to form their own models and break out in acts of "protest masculinity." MFY did not reject any of these theories, but to the contrary suggested that there was merit in all of them, and that parts of each might be usefully applied to action. The female-centered household theory might lead, for example, to concern with "the sex distribution of school faculties, the relative masculinity of curricular content, and other features of the school that might result in a definition of education as feminine."[19] Its central theory, however, was based on somewhat different assumptions about delinquent behavior, that of opportunity structure:[20]

Foremost among these is the conviction that delinquency is not simply an asocial or a "primitive" reaction. People sometimes "explain" the law-violating patterns of juvenile delinquents by suggesting that these youngsters have been inadequately socialized, poorly trained at home or school. The delinquent, they say, has simply not learned the "rights" and "wrongs" of conduct in a civilized society. We do not subscribe to explanations of this kind, for we do not view the delinquent as untouched or unreached by the society of which he is a part. It has been our experience that most persons who participate in delinquent patterns are fully aware of the differences between right and wrong, between conventional behavior and rule-violating behavior. They may not care about the differences, or they may enjoy flouting the rules of the game, or they may have decided that illegitimate practices get them what they want more efficiently than legitimate practices. But to say this is not the same as to say that they do not understand the rules.

Secondly, we believe that delinquency and conformity generally result from the same social conditions. Efforts to conform, to live up to social expectations, often result in profound strain and frustration because the opportunities for conformity are not always available. This frustration may lead in turn to behavior which violates social rules. In this way delinquency and conformity can arise from the same features of social life: unsuccessful attempts to be what one is supposed to be may lead to aberrant behavior, since the very act of reaching out for socially approved goals *under conditions that preclude their legitimate achievement* engenders strain.

Finally, we believe that delinquency ordinarily represents a search for solutions to problems of adjustment. In the sense that delinquency is an effort to resolve difficulties resulting from attempts to conform, it is not purposeless, although it may be random and disorganized and may not result in a successful solution. (In fact, delinquent "solutions" may even bring on additional and more serious problems of adjustment.)

In summary, it is our belief that much delinquent behavior is engendered because opportunities for conformity are limited. Delinquency therefore represents not a lack of motivation to conform but quite the opposite: the desire to meet social expectations itself becomes the source of delinquent behavior if the possibility of doing so is limited or nonexistent.

The importance of these assumptions in framing the large-scale program which is proposed here cannot be over-emphasized. The essence of our approach to prevention, rehabilitation, and social control in the field of juvenile delinquency may be stated as follows: in order to reduce the incidence of delinquent behavior or to rehabilitate persons who are already enmeshed in delinquent patterns, we must provide the social and psychological resources that make conformity possible.

The document is not without weaknesses. A certain gushiness comes through, in the manner of well-to-do benefactors thinking up a nicer life for the poor. For example, the coffee shop project:[21]

Three store front cultural centers will be set up within the Mobilization area, each having the outward aspect of a coffee house. An attractive new facility, symbolic of the style and mood of the youth themselves, each shop will be "jazzy" and "cool." The shops will be expressive of the socially acceptable interests of lower class youth, aged 16 to 20, and thus will provide an alternative to illegitimate patterns.

(Two years later the MFY *News Bulletin* carried a photographic "Study in Concentration" of the one coffee house that was set up: young men in blazers playing chess. Several years after that, the MFY Director allowed that the project hadn't exactly worked out as planned.)

But if a measure of fantasy found its way into the proposal, there was also present a fair-minded insistence that the MFY prospectus was after all only a set of middle-class notions of what was to be done, and that as soon as could possibly be managed, the program ideas for MFY should start coming from the people of the area itself—in cooperation with the staff, to be sure, but a staff trained and drilled to understand that the indigenous disadvantaged know more about what ails them than do social engineers from Columbia. For the fundamental fact of the MFY plan was that it proposed to mobilize not just the youth of the area, but the entire community. The plan was to energize and organize the adults of the area no less than the minor children in a coordinated effort to deal with the problems the children were facing in their effort to grow into adults.

A striking quality about the MFY proposal is the degree to which its Program for Action corresponds in structure and detail to the Economic Opportunity Act that was presented to Congress two and a quarter years later, even, indeed, to the martial spirit of their popular designations, and the actual terminology in many instances. The community action title of the Economic Opportunity Act, for example, defines such a program as one that "mobilizes" public and private resources.

| MOBILIZATION FOR YOUTH—1961 | ECONOMIC OPPORTUNITY ACT OF 1964 |
|---|---|
| *The World of Work* | Title I. *Youth Programs* |
| Urban Youth Service Corps | Part A. Job Corps Program |
| Exploratory Work Course | Part B. Work Training Programs (Neighborhood Youth Corps) |
| Youth Jobs Center . . . Other programs to overcome occupational barriers . . . Training vocational personnel | |
| *The World of Education* | Part C. *Work - Study Programs* |
| Teacher training | |
| Curriculum improvement | |
| Parent-school relations | |
| Other preschool and elementary school programs | Title II. *Operation Head Start* |
| Other guidance and personnel services | |
| *The Community* | Title II. *Community Action Agencies* |
| Organizing the unaffiliated | |
| Operation Assimilation | |
| Lower East Side Neighborhoods Association | |
| Neighborhood Councils | |

| MOBILIZATION FOR YOUTH—1961 | ECONOMIC OPPORTUNITY ACT OF 1964 |
|---|---|
| *Specialized Services to Individuals and Families*<br>  Neighborhood Service Centers | Title III.<br>  *Family Unity Through Jobs*<br>  Comprehensive Service Centers (Title II) |
| *Specialized Services to Groups*<br>  Coffee-Shop Project<br>  Detached Worker Project<br>  The Adventure Corps |   Urban and rural cooperatives<br>  VISTA (Volunteers In Service to America)<br>Title III.<br>  *Special Programs to Combat Poverty in Rural Areas* |
| *Preadolescent Project*<br>  Other services to groups | Title IV.<br>  Employment and Investment Incentives |
| (Not every proposed MFY project is included in this list.) | (Not all programs listed were specified in the EAO of 1964.) |

The central concept of each program is that of opportunity, which indeed became the key term in the title of the Federal act. The significance of this particular similarity is strengthened by the fact that the choice of the term was in ways happenstance. For most of the period of its development the Economic Opportunity Act was officially termed the Human Resources Development Act of 1964. The final title was suggested by James L. Sundquist, then Deputy Under Secretary of Agriculture. Sec. 2 of the Act, declaring that "It is therefore the policy of the United States to eliminate the paradox of poverty in the midst of plenty in this Nation by opening to everyone the opportunity for education and training, the opportunity to work, and the opportunity to live in decency and dignity," was written by Christopher Weeks, a Shriver aide. This was in turn an adaptation of the Preamble to the draft specifications of the Bill to Combat Poverty drawn up in the White House and circulated within the government on January 21, 1964, which spoke of providing everyone, especially youth, "a full opportunity to break the chains of hopeless poverty which have been passed on from generation to generation." It is to be doubted that there was any conscious use of MFY terminology here. The more important fact is that the idea of expanding *opportunities* had suffused the Washington atmosphere, just as it had suffused that of New York in which the MFY program had been conceived. Similarly, the two programs not only corresponded in detail, but in the priorities assigned to the various proposed activities. The first issue to be joined, both in combatting delinquency and warring on poverty, was that of jobs for young people. The second was education for young people. Only then came community action, and thereafter services to special groups such as farmers, small businessmen, and the like. These were ideas that made sense to people in the 1950's and early 1960's.

1961 was an exciting year in America: change was in the wind; new ideas were being sought. Here, in the MFY proposal, was as stimulating and comprehensive a set as could be hoped for. Not surprisingly, within six months a singular consortium consisting of the Ford Foundation, the City of New York, and the Federal government was put together to provide a three year, $12.5 million grant. In round terms, Ford put up 15 per cent, the City of New York 30 per cent, and the rest came from Washington. The National Institute of Mental Health contributed 36 per cent, the President's Committee on Juvenile Delinquency and Youth Crime 16 per cent, with the Labor Department and other agencies providing the remainder. (With the passage of the Manpower Development and Training Act of 1962, the Labor Department contribution rose considerably.) This was social experimentation on a large

58

scale. From the outset it was understood that what came to pass in those thirteen census tracts on the Lower East Side would have national significance. The program was launched in a sunny ceremony in the White House garden on May 31, 1962. The official nature of the undertaking was made clear: the Ford Foundation's jujitsu was at work. The Democratic Party, the Chief Executive of the nation, and the mayor of its largest city were sponsoring the project. "New York's program," the President declared, "is the best in the country at this time, and is the furthest along." He thanked the Members of Congress who had worked on this problem of juvenile delinquency, which, he added, "is really perhaps not the most descriptive phrase; it's really a question of young people and their opportunity—." The President beamed. Mayor Wagner squinted. In the background the Attorney General, chairman of the President's Committee on Juvenile Delinquency and Youth Crime, had a quizzical look. But this was no moment for doubts.

## NOTES

1. Peter Marris and Martin Rein, *Dilemmas of Social Reform, Poverty and Community Action in the United States* (New York: Atherton Press, 1967), p. 20.

2. *Ibid.* p. 44. Ylvisaker is quoted from an address to the National Council on Community Foundations, May 1964, entitled "Private Philanthropy in America."

3. *Ibid.*, p. 54

4. *Ibid.*, p. 53

5. Lloyd E. Ohlin, "Issues in the Development of Indigenous Social Movements Among Residents of Deprived Urban Areas," 1960, mimeographed.

6. Richard A. Cloward and Lloyd E. Ohlin, *Delinquency and Opportunity: A Theory of Delinquent Gangs* (New York: Free Press, 1960).

7. U. S. Department of Health, Education, and Welfare, *Re-*

*port to the Congress on Juvenile Delinquency* (Washington, D.C.: U.S. Government Printing Office, 1960).

8. Travis Hirschi and Hanan C. Selvin, "False Criteria of Casuality in Delinquency Research," *Social Problems,* Winter 1966.

9. *Ibid.,* pp. 257, 268.

10. Nisbet, *op. cit.,* p. 14.

11. Melvin Seeman, "On the Meaning of Alienation," *American Sociological Review,* 24, (1959), pp. 783–791.

12. For a masterful summary, see Melvin Seeman, "Social Cohesion, Social Structure and Alienation," Social Report of the President, forthcoming. See also R. Jessor *et al., Society, Personality and Deviant Behavior* (New York: Holt, Rinehart and Winston, 1968).

13. Robert K. Merton. *Contemporary Social Problems; An Introduction to the Sociology of Deviant Behavior and Social Disorganization.* Edited by Robert K. Merton and Robert A. Nisbet, (New York: Harcourt, Brace & World, 1961).

14. Robert K. Merton, *Social Theory and Social Structure,* Enlarged Edition (New York: Free Press. 1968, pp. 215–248).

15. Mobilization For Youth, Inc., *A Proposal for the Prevention and Control of Delinquency by Expanding Opportunities.* (New York: Mobilization for Youth, Inc., 1961).

16. *Ibid.,* p. iv.

17. *Ibid.,* p. vi.

18. *Ibid.,* p. viii.

19. *Ibid.,* p. 43.

20. *Ibid.,* p. 43–45.

21. *Ibid.,* p. 164.

# CHAPTER FOUR

# THE PRESIDENT'S COMMITTEE ON JUVENILE DELINQUENCY AND YOUTH CRIME

The disposition of government is toward continuity. The 1960 Children's Bureau-NIMH report on juvenile delinquency may have had its methodological failings, but its proposal (incorporated in departmental legislation already several times proposed to the Congress, but as yet not acted upon) that the Federal government undertake a series of research and demonstration projects in this field was there waiting for the Kennedy administration when it took office. Embellished, but only that, by the exhilarating style and glamorous personalities of the New Frontier, this is what happened.

Juvenile delinquency had not been an issue in the Presidential campaign. Kennedy mentioned the subject only twice during the long journey of August 1 through November 7, and on neither occasion did he indicate that he had been influenced by the newest thinking on the subject. In Indianapolis, oblivious, apparently, to the research of Herbert Gans and others on the effects of urban renewal on community cohesion, he asked (referring to Republican delinquencies), "How can you measure the cost of juvenile delinquency in the slums which have not been torn down by an effective urban renewal program?" In Pittsburgh, ostensibly indifferent to the new style in social change, he pointed with scorn to the Republican record, "On alleviating juvenile delinquency—research it." Nonetheless, this seemingly humdrum, marginal subject happened to involve the two most pressing domestic issues that were to face the Kennedy administration: employment and race. At the moment Kennedy took office, five and one-half Americans were without jobs—the highest number since the Great Depression. Save for a brief period in 1958, insured unemployment was at the highest point in its history. This was the first subject with which he dealt in his State of the Union address, January 30, 1961.

> We take office in the wake of seven months of recession, three and one-half years of slack, seven years of diminished economic growth, and nine years of falling farm income.

The unemployment rates for youth were twice those for the work force as a whole, and among Negro youth these rates routinely attained levels that must be described as horrendous. Although the economy turned up the month after Kennedy took office, employment lagged behind. Further, it seemed to be acquiring patterns sharply inhospitable to the poor, notably the Negro poor fleeing the depressed countryside.

Although the economists within the government, especially those in the Bureau of Labor Statistics, did not see any great signs of the work force being wiped out by automation, the terms was nonetheless on everyone's lips. Many public men, including some in the administration, were convinced that the job problem was not going to be solved. (In an article published shortly after the assassination, Hans J. Morgenthau listed "permanent unemployment" as one of the legacies of the Kennedy era.) At all events, it did not appear that conventional economic processes would do the trick: for example, between 1957 and 1963, *all* of the increase in employment in the United States was accounted for by jobs added to the public sector.

Although the level, or visibility, of Negro protest was not especially high at this time, it steadily mounted in the months that followed, and frequently focused on unemployment as an issue. This reflected the gradual urbanization and secularization of the movement, and the influence of socialist thinkers such as Bayard Rustin. The 1963 March on Washington was for "Jobs and Freedom." The connection between race problems and economic problems was obvious enough. Moreover, at this time it was just barely beginning to be perceived that social conditions in the slums of the large cities were inching towards instability. In retrospect it would appear they were in fact galloping in that direction; but if no one fully realized that, at least the direction was noted. For one thing, the implications of the unnerving rate of youth crime among urban Negroes was beginning to be grasped. Any set of propositions that connected these phenomena, which is precisely what the opportunity theory did, had a built-in audience in the Kennedy administration—not only an audience but a partisan in the person of the President's brother, the Attorney General. The stages by which Robert Kennedy's interest in this field developed must await his biographer. It is sufficient for this narrative that he was Attorney General and in that capacity formally concerned with matters of law enforcement. And further he was just then beginning the steady escalation of his involvement with the life of the poor, perhaps especially the Negro poor, that was to be the dominant passion of his life at the end.

Juvenile delinquency was, moreover, increasingly a political problem about which an American political leader was required at this time at least to appear to be concerned. Kennedy touched on the subject in his first State of the Union Address, "Organized and juvenile crimes cost the taxpayers millions of dollars each year, making it essential that we have improved enforcement and new legislative safeguards." In his first press conference, May Craig asked about the subject. The administration responded. David Hackett, a close boyhood friend of Robert F. Kennedy's (he was to be one of his pall bearers) and an important aide in the 1960 campaign, was made special assistant to the Attorney General, and told to work up something. With no experience in the field, Hackett was open to new ideas. Almost immediately he was visited by representatives of the Ford Foundation, Dyke Brown, a senior executive, and David Hunter, a person of energy, intelligence, and devotion to social change, who was responsible for MFY affairs at Ford. The theory of MFY was expounded to Hackett, with perhaps a special emphasis on the coordination functions stressed by the grey area projects. It took. On May 11, 1961, the President sent a message to Congress reporting an apparent increase in delinquency, which "seems to occur most often among school drop-outs and unemployed youth faced with limited opportunities and from broken families." He proposed that the Federal government undertake projects to "demonstrate and evaluate" the most effective countermeasures: "Measures must be taken to reach deeply into the experiences of every-day life in deprived families and local communities." In the meantime, he was establishing by Executive Order a committee made up of the Attorney General, the Secretary of Health, Education, and Welfare, and the Secretary of Labor "to coordinate their efforts in the development of a program of Federal leadership to assist the states and local communities."

The appointment of the President's Committee on Juvenile Delinquency and Youth Crime was decisive. As the President's statement of May 11th indicated, the key concepts were there at the outset: "opportunity," "coordination," "community." Key men in the government took up the matter. The Attorney General, by virtue of his rank in the cabinet, of the nature of the subject, and of his personal position in the administration, became chairman. In Arthur Goldberg at Labor and Abraham Ribicoff at HEW he had personal friends and political allies for colleagues. The committee began work with a small sum from White House funds. David Hackett was made executive director of PCJD, as it came to be designated. Hackett, a steady, pleasant man with a well-developed capacity for listening to others and an easily underestimated capacity to persist in an enterprise once begun, gathered a vibrant group around him. This included Lloyd Ohlin, a scholar at once self-effacing and immensely persuasive; Sanford L. Kravitz, a warm, tough, experienced social worker-intellectual; and Richard Boone of the Public Affairs Department of the Ford Foundation. Boone thereupon became a decisive actor in the drama of community action. A deceptively bland, seemingly unassertive professional, he had done graduate work in sociology at the University of Chicago where he had thoroughly absorbed the tradition of community organization which the renowned Chicago sociologists of 1920's and 1930's had taken off-campus, into their environs. He thus brought to the theories of the Columbia School of Social Work a legacy of applied practice going back three decades and more. In the end, when all others had left, Boone was still practicing.

The group was primarily influenced by the theoretical perceptions of Cloward and Ohlin, but also those of Albert K. Cohen, whose study, *Delinquent Boys: The Culture of the Gang,* proposed the not dissimilar view of "the origins of delinquency among lower-class youth as less a failure of personality than a failure in the opportunity structure."[1] In September, Congress enacted the Juvenile Delinquency and Youth Offences Control Act, providing for demonstration and training projects in "the most effective ways of using total resources to combat juvenile delinquency in local communities." Ten million dollars a year for three years was authorized. The Federal government, the President asserted, had become an active partner in dealing with a national concern that required national action.

For a period, the committee, or rather its irrepressible staff, was a force of great influence within the government, waging war on the bureaucracy, attracting ideas and men from the outside, and colonizing them within the government. They sometimes referred to themselves as "the guerillas." A new technique of program development was conceived: a package of Federal services provided to select communities as part of an antideliquency program. The new administration had only limited funds for new programs, but large and visible enterprises could be assembled by combining bits and pieces of ongoing programs; some education money from HEW, some training money from

Labor, some Housing money from HHFA, and so on. With the President's brother to encourage cooperation, the PCJD staff set out to assemble such packages.

Sanford L. Kravitz, a member of the committee staff and later Chief of Research and Program Development in the Community Action Program of OEO, has described the process as follows:[2]

As a criteria for the receipt of funds, communities were asked to indicate how they would plan for the attack on the problem, which was defined as primarily rooted in the social structure, requiring both interdisciplinary professional attention, as well as a multifaceted program approach which simultaneously addressed the many causes of delinquency. In addition, since key institutions, both public and voluntary, would have to be involved, each community was asked either to develop a new organizational structure which combined these elements or to regroup existing agencies.

. . . The criteria for effective programs stressed certain critical elements:

1. The interrelationship of social problems.
2. Emphasis on remedies that focused on institutional change rather than on redirection of personality.
3. Intensive effort toward problem definition, formulation of a conceptual base for solutions, and development of programs which would take off from that base.
4. Recognition of the necessity for substantial participation of political government in the efforts to be undertaken.

From the outset, in the MFY pattern, the Ford Foundation was frequently on the scene, working alongside the PCJD. The two organizations used their leverage on others. The New Haven program, which the President announced in a White House ceremony October, 1963, and which he described as "the beginning of a very significant Federal program to cooperate with States, local communities, and private organizations in a major attack on the problems facing our youth," was financed, in addition to contributions from Ford and the PCJD, by grants from a local foundation, the local school board, the local Redevelopment Agency, and three Federal agencies.

Everywhere the two organizations went, the first visible consequence of the delinquency program was a new community organization. Kravitz has observed that the simultaneous (and clearly interrelated) entry of the Federal government and the nation's largest foundation into the business of institutional change "not only jolted the communities into which they were moved but also spread reverberating shock waves throughout most of the medium-sized and larger communities of the nation. [The] existing pattern of planning for and coordinating social services was being sharply challenged."[3] The reaction among welfare professionals was mixed: for some the new and incipient community agencies became "shining symbols of what might be done." For others, he notes, they represented "a monstrous compound of evil, waste, and, most heinous of all, disrespect for experience." The latter point is not to be ignored: for all the social idealism involved, the new programs were not without an element of youth displacing age. But then, that was very much the political style of the moment, a not unrelated fact. Perhaps the real message delivered by the President's committee and the Ford Foundation was that the big guns were moving in on a problem, or collection of problems, that had at best been a marginal affair concerning marginal people. This, moreover, was not just an impression; it was so.

The fact that this was so received perhaps heightened attention from another circumstance: despite the air of innovation and unreality of the delinquency program, not that much else was going on in Washington. The Kennedy legislative program got off to a slow start and was never particularly successful until after his death. Even near-certain measures such as the Manpower Development and Training Act, which had been expected within the early months of the Eighty-seventh Congress, took more than a year to be enacted, longer to be funded, and longer yet to be put into the field. By contrast, the PCJD was on the ground early, moved fast, cost little, had friends in high places—as good a formula for success in Washington as any.

In its relatively short life as one of the glamorous institutions of a new and vital administration (with the death of Kennedy the program more or less reverted to its technical status of a small operation in HEW), the President's Committee did not in truth get a great many community action programs into actual operation; the planning process took time, and was intended to take time. But a good deal was learned, and almost all of it seemed at the time to confirm the theoretical foundations on which the planning went forward. Kravitz suggests that the PCJD activity threw lights on seven problems: [4]

1. Many voluntary "welfare programs were not reaching the poor."
2. If they were reaching the poor, the services offered were often inappropriate.
3. Services aimed at meeting the needs of disadvantaged people were typically fragmented and unrelated.
4. Realistic understanding by professionals and community leaders of the problems faced by the poor was limited.
5. Each specialty field was typically working in encapsulated fashion on a particular kind of problem, without awareness of the other fields or of efforts toward interlock.
6. There was little political leadership involvement

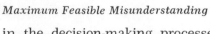

in the decision-making processes of voluntary social welfare.

7. There was little or no serious participation of program beneficiaries in programs being planned and implemented by professionals and elite community leadership.

It is important to note that the last problem Kravitz touches upon—the problem of the poor participating in programs designed for their benefit—was preceded by another problem, namely, that political leaders—City Hall—did not seem much involved either. This is a crucial point. The staff of the President's Committee were themselves at the very heart of the government establishment and had not the least thought of bringing about through their work political upheavals that might embarrass, much less disestablish the existing order. They wished the poor to be involved in the program, but in the interests of therapy as much as anything else. They also wanted City Hall involved. They were reformers. They cared about those who were suffering and poor. They wanted others also to become involved so that they too would care, and in particular they wanted to involve those who had the power to do something about the suffering and the poverty. It was as simple and decent as that.

Given the interdepartmental structure of the President's Committee, the fact that its staff director identified his concerns with those of the Administration itself, and perhaps also the fact that it really had no money worth speaking of and few administrative chores, it was inevitable that it should widen its concerns. In fairly short order, from being concerned with delinquency it came to be involved with the entire question of poverty, rather as the administration itself

<u>did.</u> In a memorandum to the Attorney General written November 6, 1963, Hackett described the process:[5]

> In our work on the Juvenile Delinquency program, we have learned that programs for the prevention and control of delinquency must deal not only with the delinquent, but also with disadvantaged youths who may become delinquent unless there is substantial intervention on their behalf. Such an approach is broad, encompassing many young people, and concentrating on their environment—the family, the school, the local labor market, etc.
>
> This comprehensive approach precludes the use of traditional concepts and plans which call for dealing merely with the delinquent in uncoordinated programs. It requires the development of new opportunities for the disadvantaged youth and change in the institutions which affect them. To create this kind of program, the President's Committee has encouraged local planning, leading to a coordination of resources for a total attack on the problems of disadvantaged youth.
>
> . . . Because of the intimate relationship between poverty and crime our comprehnsive programs of delinquency prevention and control have inevitably led to attempts to deal with poverty and its effects. The Juvenile Delinquency program has emphasized access to opportunity for youth as a way of combatting poverty; thus, the Juvenile Delinquency program has, in fact, concentrated its resources on attacks on poverty in selected target cities.

This would at first appear to be the purest Cloward-Ohlin doctrine, but at this point yet another element had entered into the thinking of Hackett and the group of young officials he had gathered around him. <u>This was the notion of a "Domestic Peace Corps" that would carry out in the impoverished regions and neighborhoods of the United States much the same functions that the Peace Corps itself performed overseas.</u> Fairly early, Hackett had begun holding regular meetings of the "guerillas," young, bright, energetic New Frontiersmen, with an important sprinkling of career professionals, whose interests ranged far and wide over the problems of poverty, race, urban affairs, indeed

7 1

the entire domestic scene.[6] At this moment in time perhaps *the* great success of the Kennedy administration was the Peace Corps. In one master concept it had brought together the most divergent of impulses and attractions—missionary zeal, the junior year abroad, youthful idealism, no-nonsense pragmatism, the thirst for adventure, government medical care, and a watchful American consul. It was (and is) a program almost exclusively designed for well-educated middle-class youth, and involves not an inconsiderable subvention for them. (The average Peace Corps volunteer requires an annual government outlay of $7,832:[7] more than the Job Corps.) But no doubt for that very reason it was immensely popular with the middle-class media. Further, Leonard Duhl observes, it "proved the theory that well motivated, non-professional people could direct themselves and thus their efforts to the critical issues found in overseas communities."[8] It was inevitable that the notion of applying the same technique to domestic problems should arise, as indeed it did among the "guerillas." On November 11, 1962, President Kennedy established a cabinet level study group to draw up a program for a National Service Corps, as it was tentatively known. The chairman of the group was the Attorney General, and the floating staff that gathered in a dilapidated Lafayette Square town house that served for headquarters was substantially the staff of the President's Committee on Juvenile Delinquency and Youth Crime.

What emerged from the group's planning effort was a program for community action: the Peace Corps concept brought home. Although the Peace Corps itself was new, the concept of "community development" had been a central element of the foreign aid program from its inception. Applying it in the United States, particularly in regions such as Appalachia, an area with which the Kennedy Administration was particularly concerned, seemed at the time abundantly sensible, although this may or may not have been so. The problem of communities assisted by the foreign aid program are typically not those of social integration, or social alienation, but rather of technological backwardness. Part at least of this backwardness is characteristically the result of *too much* community cohesion, that is, the grip of tradition, rather than otherwise. Even so, in a Special Message to the Congress on the Nation's Youth, sent February 14, 1963, President Kennedy proposed the establishment of a National Service Corps, a direct counterpart of the overseas Peace Corps, designed to complement the Youth Employment Act in providing opportunities and services to the one-sixth of the population living at a submarginal level:

This small task force of men and women will work in locally-planned and initiated projects, at the invitation of community institutions, and under local supervision.

As with the Ford Foundation projects, and those of the PCJD, the need for outside intervention to appear locally initiated, was always in view. That there was an element of deception in this posture—that it was altogether deception—should not be doubted.

*NOTES*

1. Albert K. Cohen, *Delinquent Boys; The Culture of the Gang* (New York: The Free Press, 1963).
2. Sanford L. Kravitz, "The Community Action Program: Past-Present-Future," mimeographed, 1965.
3. *Ibid.*
4. *Ibid.*

5. Quoted in Herbert Krosney, *Beyond Welfare, Poverty in the Supercity* (New York: Holt, Rinehart, and Winston, 1966) p. 9.

6. Among them were Sanford L. Kravitz, Frederick O'R. Hayes, and Leonard J. Duhl.

7. As of 1966.

8. Leonard J. Duhl, M.D., "Some Origins of the Poverty Program," mimeographed, p. 3.

# CHAPTER FIVE

# THE WAR
# ON POVERTY

The *élan* and patronage of the President's Committee on Juvenile Delinquency and Youth Crime ought not to lead to the assumption that the program was necessarily successful. Indeed, on balance it would appear it was not. The match was unequal. The concept of the "guerrillas"—living off the administrative countryside, invisible to the bureaucratic enemy but known to one another, hitting and running and making off with the riches of the established departments—was attractive, but also romantic. Simply as a matter of firepower, God was on the side of the big battalions. The smaller ones, such as the Children's Bureau could bide their time. (Within three to four years of the height of their activities, it would appear that not a single member of the guerrillas was still in government. Certainly the group had ceased to operate by 1965.) But just as important, it might well be judged that the group had only a weak understanding of the problems with which it sought to deal. At once condescending and naïve, it was ahead of its time perhaps, but not nearly abreast of its subject.

Marris and Rein conclude that the PCJD administrative structure in Washington failed. The hoped-for programs did not materialize in anything like the expected dimensions:[1]

> The delinquency programme operated, then through an unstable alliance of Robert Kenndy's personal authority with internal departmental rivalries, and the mutual understanding of a small group of idealistic innovators within the bureaucracy. The interlocking cadres of professional staff, who were to represent the President's Committee policies in each department and co-ordinate Federal resources, were never satisfactorily established. As a formal administrative rationalization within the Federal government the plan failed. The direction of policy and its implementation were never integrated, and the politically minded staff of the Committee maintained at best an uneasy relationship with the more professional departments.

Moreover, it would appear that even the research effort came to little. The Ford Foundation, as Marris and Rein note, stressed "institutional coherence," seeking a new coalition of community leadership; while the *quest of the PCJD,* in its professional aspect, was for "intellectual coherence . . . a proven theory of social rehabilitation.[2]

The program early on ran into trouble with Congress, notably with the redoubtable Edith Green who very much took the lead in educational matters in the merged House Committee on Education and Labor. Repeatedly she made clear that the legislative mandate of the PCJD was not to reform urban society, nor yet to try out the sociological theories of Émile Durkheim on

American youth: the legislative mandate was to reduce juvenile delinquency. To essay more was to trifle
with Congressional intent. The long months of research
design and project preparation, the unfamiliar terminology, were received with suspicion and increasing
hostility on Capitol hill.[3]

Not so in the Bureau of the Budget. In a subtle, not
entirely clear process, the coordinated community approach to problems of the poor attracted great interest
and ultimately powerful and crucial support in that
nerve center, indeed superego, of the Federal establishment. Something about the style of the President's
committee appealed both to the immediate preoccupations and the deep concerns—they might also be called
longings—of the budget examiners whose job it is to
give some order and direction to the bewildering array
of domestic programs that steadily accumulate, under
Republicans and Democrats, popular and unpopular
Presidents, reactionary or liberal congresses. The job
of the Bureau of the Budget is to make the system
work. "Coordination" is the ever-invoked, but never-
achieved ideal: a system that would work with harmony and efficiency, that would protect the interests
of the President, carry out the intent of Congress, and,
if possible, get the most for the taxpayer's dollar. Trying to do this is a frustrating job at best: in ways it is
an effort to do something that cannot be done, it being
the plight of government bureaucracy, as James Q.
Wilson has shown, to have such conflicting demands
imposed upon it by the public as to create rather strict
limits to how much it can achieve, and especially, how
readily it can produce innovations in its own operations or respond to innovations elsewhere. Just to keep
up with what is going on becomes increasingly difficult.
True coordination, especially at the pinnacle of the
system in Washington, is difficult if not impossible.

America is too big, too far away. It would appear that in the community action agency a number of the leading budget examiners in the Bureau perceived the alluring, intoxicating possibility of doing it from the *bottom*. Moreover, the President's committee approach had many other features that were remarkably attractive to the Bureau. It was as if someone were finally listening to them: the emphasis on planning (recall that Mobilization for Youth took four and one-half years just to draw up a program proposal) and on coordinating services; the insistence on the interrelationship of things; and probably not least, the determination to keep track of what happened, to measure results, and to learn from the experience, had the strongest appeal to the Bureau. "Evaluation" was a central concern of all the delinquency programs. Early in the program social scientists from across the nation met at Annapolis to confer on the techniques for assessing the expected results. Provisions for this most elusive (and as it turned out unsuccessful) effort were built into the specifications of each of the PCJD programs. It would appear that increasingly the Bureau of the Budget saw in the new social invention, the community action agency, a means to impose order and efficiency on the chaos of government programs that had descended on the American city. Order and efficiency are not small matters in the eyes of the Bureau of the Budget.

It may be that at this time in Washington the need was especially evident. If Kennedy was not getting all he asked for in the way of legislation, he was nonetheless asking for a very great deal. The interdepartmental bargaining and squabbling that preceded the submission of new legislation gave promise of open warfare should the programs be enacted. These struggles were, and are, more on the minds of the staff of the Executive Office of the President than perhaps of any other group. In the Ford Foundation, in the intellectuals and activists surrounding the President's Committee, there seemed at last to have come into being a group that understood this issue and was seeking institutional devices to cope with it. The receptivity of the Bureau of the Budget and the Council of Economic Advisors to these ideas at this time was probably further enhanced by the somewhat special quality of the men assigned to work on the antipoverty program. In a milieu of accustomed excellence, these men—William Cannon, William Capron, Michael March, Charles Schultze, Burton Wiesbrod—were especially distinguished. Close to universities, intellectual by bent, familiar with social science beyond the confines of economics, in them the sponsors of community action could not have hoped for more perceptive arbiters.

The influence of the PCJD and the Ford Foundation is to be encountered at the very outset of the planning of the poverty program. A Council of Economic Advisors Staff Memorandum of October 29, 1963—almost a month before the assassination—entitled "Program for a Concerted Assault on Poverty," set forth in detail the concept of The Poverty Cycle and the need for "a coordinated attack" to break the cycle through preventive, rehabilitative, and ameliorative interventions. (It may be noted, however, that the poverty cycle was at this point still seen almost solely in terms of the individual, whose "cultural and environmental obstacles to motivation" led to "poor health, and inadequate education, and low mobility limiting earning potential" which in turn led to "limited income opportunities," which resulted in "poverty," which led to poor motivation, and so around again.)

The following day, Walter W. Heller, Chairman of the Council of Economic Advisors, wrote members of the cabinet asking for proposals that "might be woven into a basic attack on poverty and waste of human resources, as part of the 1964 legislative program." The proposals, when they arrived, were disappointing to the committee that had been set up in the Executive Office Building to direct the operation. The Bureau of the Budget thereupon requested Hackett to submit a proposal, which he did in a set of memoranda proposing that the available funds ($500 million had been tentatively assigned to the new program) be devoted to a series of comprehensive community action programs. These were in effect the juvenile delinquency programs taken just a bit further in scope and resources.

Hackett's proposal was accepted. It responded fully to the concerns, fears, hopes, expectations of the quasi-permanent presidential staff "across the street" from the White House and was quickly adopted by his personal staff in the West Wing—which, it may be noted, continued for some time under Johnson to be made up largely of Kennedy men. Theodore C. Sorenson, Myer Feldman, and Lee C. White, who were successively Special Counsel to the President and in turn handled the antipoverty legislation, were all Kennedy appointees. Whether this enhanced the reception of a proposal coming from the Attorney General's office, and whether it subsequently affected President Johnson's reaction to the program as enacted, it is not possible to say with certainty, but the presumption must be that it did. Few things that Robert Kennedy had touched were not thereafter viewed with suspicion, fear, and distaste by the staff of the Johnson White House, and of course most of all by the President himself.

Nonetheless, President Johnson went ahead with the Kennedy-conceived program. In his State of the Union Message for 1964, he proclaimed the war on poverty and went on to declare that "the central problem is to protect and restore man's satisfaction in belonging to a community where he can find security and significance." The principal drafter of the message was Richard N. Goodwin, whose ties to Robert F. Kennedy now grew even stronger.

On January 21, 1964, Lee White, then Assistant Special Counsel sent to the Secretaries of Labor, Agriculture, HEW, Commerce, Interior, the Attorney General, and the Administration of the Housing and Home Finance Agency "the draft specifications for the poverty bill."

*Title:* To authorize assistance for Community Action Programs to combat poverty.

The purpose of the act would be as follows:

[To] conduct an all-out, continuous, sustained war on poverty in accord with a strategy which

a. Strikes at the main front of poverty—the perpetuation and transmission of poverty, ignorance, disease, squalor and hopelessness, from one generation to another. . . .

b. Uses weapons directly aimed at improving human motivation and performance: education, vocational and work training, health services, job opportunities, a decent home in a healthy productive environment, and harmonious and stable family and community life.

c. Attacks poverty through comprehensive action programs, initiated, planned, and carried out in local communities. . . .

d. Mobilizes existing and new Federal assistance and services to support local Community Action Programs. . . .

Communities were to be given funds and twelve months to prepare their programs, which would provide the following:

[A]n effective plan and arrangement for administering the comprehensive Community Action Program—preferably through a single organization or official—with adequate power and authority to exercise comprehensive coordination of efforts to combat poverty in the area, and *with appropriate representation of and participation by the key governmental agencies, community, and neighborhood groups, and professional and other organizations in the area.* The administration of the Community Action Program will involve utilization of all relevant existing or new programs in the community—local, state, federal—but with monitoring and coordination by the community action organization and development of cooperative facilities wherever appropriate. [My italics.]

Two alternative organizational plans were put forward. Under the first, the coordinating authority for the Federal end of the program would be vested in the Secretary of HEW. (Technically, the juvenile delinquency program was an HEW operation.) Under the second, an independent director would be appointed by the President. In sum, the bill incorporated the purest doctrine. It represented the direct transmission of social science theory into governmental policy.

But it did not prevail. First, the pressure from other established departments for their programs forced the President to bring in Shriver to impose order. Then Shriver, in effect, joined the protesters. His appointment was announced February 1. The next day in a meeting at his home CEA and BOB representatives explained the idea of community action. Shriver balked. He just did not see how it would work.[4] Yarmolinsky's notes record his objection: "Where you need the money worst, you'll have the worst plans." His faith in the potential of community leadership was, at this point, limited, and declined further the next day, February 3rd, at a large meeting of his task force with other government officials and a number of outsiders, when he learned that the time it would take to produce a comprehensive community action program would preclude any dramatic results for the war on poverty in time, for example, to influence the 1964 election, or even the selection of the President's running mate.

Something more than plain politics was involved. The antipoverty program had become for many of the stricken Kennedy men of the administration a symbol of the continued viability of the New Frontier, just as for the Johnson men it was a measure of their own President's ability to take hold and lead. All concerned wanted to see results.

On February 3, 1964, the CAP advocates once more put forth their proposal. Charles Schultze explained that projects would be initiated at the local level, with a measure of federal prodding, and approved at the federal level. William Capron touched on the problem of local leadership in the South, epecially, and noted that CAP's could be used to bypass the local "power structure" with the use of Federal funds. Richard Boone insisted that the community action programs could be "manned" by the poor themselves. (Few perhaps noted Mayor Arthur Naftalin's warning not to expect too much from community leadership and his plea that new bureaucracies must not be created, that rather the existing bureaucracies must be made to work.) But the decisive factor was time. Boone stated that comprehensive community action plans would require one year plus to complete in urban areas, and perhaps more in rural ones. Ylvisaker argued that it would be possible to move more quickly into "quality areas" such as New Haven and Boston. But Wilbur Cohen, then Assistant Secretary of HEW, judged that at most ten CAP's could be fielded in 1964, with fifty in 1965, and one hundred in 1966. It seemed too slow. W. Willard Wirtz, the one cabinet officer present, kept pressing on education and jobs. Michael Harrington agreed that community action was a useful "long-range" objective, but saw jobs and training for selective service rejectees as the priority item.

The February 3rd meeting settled the matter in

Shriver's mind and had important consequences for the future of the war on poverty. Community action remained in the program, but attention shifted to other, more immediately promising, saleable, and dramatic measures. On February 5th, Yarmolinsky assigned a set of background papers to be prepared by task force members as the first stage of the task force's work (see opposite page). It will be seen that the priority given the various topics almost exactly corresponds to their sequence in the final legislation, and it can be stated that it corresponds to the sense of priority of the group at the time. (Especially with respect to the priority of jobs. On February 6th, Michael Harrington, Paul Jacobs, and Frank Mankiewicz sent a memorandum to Shriver. "If there is any single dominant problem of poverty in the U.S.," they declared, "it is that of unemployment.")

And this is what happened. Community action remained an *item* in the antipoverty program, but only that. It was no longer the program itself. There was never any question in the task force of dropping it: as Cohen had stated at the February 3rd meeting it *was* "the President's program." (Cohen, a career civil servant, was perhaps more sensitive to this point than some others present, still loyal to the dead Kennedy.) Richard Blumenthal argues that in fact the President and his personal aides had never much liked the original proposal as prepared in the Executive Office Building from memoranda by Boone anyway. The President wanted action, not planning; wanted nationwide scope, not target areas; wanted in particular to see that Negroes got something fast, without in the process alarming whites. As a result, by February there was little life left in the notion of picking, say, ten cities, and spending several years preparing them for the experiment.[5]

## BACKGROUND PAPERS FOR ANTIPOVERTY PROJECT*
*(Economic Independence Project? Economic Initiative Project?)*

| PROJECT | ASSIGNED TO |
|---|---|
| 1. *Jobs* | Daniel P. Moynihan |
|     Draft Rejectees. | |
|     Simple jobs for old people. | |
|     Dependent mothers (and note day care item under No. 2 below). | |
|     Other projects worth considering. | |
| 2. *Education* | Wilbur Cohen |
|     Loan funds (high school and college). | |
|     Plan to provide part-time jobs for students who cannot attend school because of need to support families (suggestion was they spend c. 10 hours a week tutoring dropouts). | |
|     Preschool age care. | |
|     Remedial reading. | |
|     Lighted school house. | |
|     Urban boarding schools. | |
|     Any other proposals. | |
| 3. *Work-study programs* | Richard Boone |
| 4. *Child health programs* | Wilbur Cohen (or his designee) |
| 5. *Community action* | Richard Boone and/or Paul N. Ylvisaker |
| 6. *Rural Programs* | James Sundquist |
| 7. *Future Jobs* (to be suggested in in the message and explored during the first year of the program) | Richard Goodwin |
| 8. *Organization of the Office* (to be set up under the statute) | Charles Schultze |
| 9. *Draft statute* | Norbert A. Schlei |
| 10. *Message* | ———— |

* Yarmolinsky's memorandum of February 5, 1964.

Although memory too readily deceives, it may be of use to record here the impression that community action simply was not much on the minds of those who were most active in the Shriver task force. In retrospect, at least, it would seem to have assumed a kind of residual function. A number of large, specific programs were going to be included in the poverty package. There would be a Job Corps for drop-outs and obviously marginal youth, a Neighborhood Youth Corps for young persons still in high school and hoping to remain there, a work-study program to assist college youth continue their studies. Unemployed fathers of dependent children would be given special training, small farmers and small business assisted, VISTA volunteers recruited and sent forth. These were the big items. In addition, it came to be assumed that there would be any number of smaller undertakings that local communities might think up and want to try out. There would be money for this in the community action title. It came to be seen not as a matter of community *action* at all, but rather as a form of community *option*.

What about Negroes in the South? Federal regulations could easily enough ensure that they would have their share, or something approaching it, of the categorical programs such as those of Title I. But what of community action, where local option would decide how to spend the new Federal money? Inasmuch as the local white power structure would control the allocation of community action money, how could it be ensured that impoverished Negroes would get something like a proportionate share? The task force, which by the third week in February was beginning to think in terms of a draft bill, came up with the equally obvious answer: provide for it in the legislation. The January 21 White House draft had provided for "appropriate representation of and participation by the key governmental agencies, community, and neighborhood groups, and key professional and other organizations in the area." This envisaged, presumably, something more than the local United Fund organization, something less than a formal incorporation of the power structure along syndicalist lines. But the one thing it did *not* provide for was the poor, especially the Southern Negro poor who, whatever else their qualities, certainly were not organized. A simple idea occurred to someone present: Why not include language that would require the poor to participate, much as it was provided that other entities should do so? Then, later, if in a given locale it became clear that Negroes were not sharing—that is, participating—in the benefits of the new program, Washington could intervene on grounds that the requirements of the legislation were not being met. The drafting committee came up with a solution. The community action title, which established the one portion of the program that would not be directly monitored from Washington, should provide for the "*maximum feasible participation of the residents of the areas and the members of the groups*" involved in the local programs (my italics). Subsequently this phrase was taken to sanction a specific theory of social change, and there were those present in Washington at the time who would have drafted just such language with precisely that object. But the record, such as can be had, and recollection indicates that it was intended to do no more than ensure that persons excluded from the political process in the South and elsewhere would nonetheless participate in the *benefits* of the community action programs of the new legislation. It was taken as a matter beneath notice that such programs would be dominated by the local political structure.

This decision was made February 23 at a meeting chaired by Yarmolinsky. Overnight, Schlei and a Justice Department group produced the first task force draft of the "Human Resources Development Act of 1964." Title I, Youth Opportunity Programs, provided for the National Youth Opportunity Corps, and a Hometown Youth Opportunity Program. (A note on the innocence of the times: it was provided that the age of selective service registration be lowered to 17 in order that rejectees could be identified earlier and provided places in the Corps.) Title II provided for Urban and Rural Community Action Programs. Title III provided Special Programs to Combat Poverty in Rural Areas. Title IV specified Employment and Investment Incentives in three parts, loans to create jobs for the long-term unemployed, small business loans, and community work and training programs for unemployed fathers and other members of needy families with children. Title V provided for a Human Resources Development Agency, authorized, among other things, to recruit volunteers to work in poverty areas.

The Community Action title was purely service oriented. A CAP was defined in Sec. 202(b) as one

(1) which mobilizes and utilizes the public and private resources of a community in a comprehensive attack on poverty;

(2) which provides services, assistance, and other activities of sufficient variety, scope, and magnitude to give promise of progress toward elimination of poverty through improving human performance, motivation, and productivity, and

(3) which is developed and conducted with the maximum feasible participation of residents of the areas and members of the groups referred to. . . .

Fourteen varieties of program particulars were referred to as examples of community action, moving from employment to education ("establish programs for the benefit of preschool children"), to health, and then to housing. In Title V, heads of other Federal departments and agencies were directed, "to the extent feasible" to give preference to applications for benefits received from community action programs. There was but one reference to the Ylvisaker-Cottrell thesis of community competence. (Leonard S. Cottrell, Jr., Secretary of the Russell Sage Foundation, had become Chairman, Citizens Advisory Council to President's Commission on Juvenile Delinquency and Youth Crime.) Sec. 204(e) of Title II provided:

In extending assistance under this section the Administrator shall give special consideration to programs which give promise of effecting a permanent increase in the capacity of individuals, groups, and communities to deal with their problems without further assistance.

The bill continued to be tinkered with. Its designation was changed to that of the Economic Opportunity Act of 1964; the term Job Corps was invented. HEW's Work-Study program providing aid for college students was put up front as Title I, Part C, so that the legislation began with a nice continuum of youth assistance programs. But marginal matters aside, the bill as introduced on March 16, 1964, and as signed into law August 20th was almost exactly the one that emerged from the first task force drafting session of February 23–24. In particular, *the participation clause was not touched.* Sec. 202(a)(3) of H.R. 10440, introduced by Congressman Phillip M. Landrum, March 16, 1964, defined a CAP in exactly the language of the task force:

(3) which is developed, conducted and administered with the maximum feasible participation of residents of the areas and members of the groups referred to. . . .

Sec. 202(a)(3) of S. 2642 introduced by Senator Pat McNamara, which passed the Senate July 23, and was signed by the President August 20, 1964, contains precisely this language, save that the final words "referred to" are replaced by "served." The only significant change in the Title II made by Congress was an addition of a Part B providing for an adult basic education program which Congressman Carl Perkins, the second-ranking Democratic member of the committee, hoped to get for his Appalachian constituents, but which was being stymied in the Rules Committee. In the manner of the Executive Departments in January and February, he tacked it onto the antipoverty package.

And that is about what there is to report. Community action had receded from the concerns of the political executives in the administration; Shriver was already caught up with the fascination of the Job Corps, while elsewhere the old-line departments were preoccupied with their "pieces of the action." This attitude was reflected in the Congressional hearings and debates. Title II was vague enough to prompt a considerable number of inquiries as to just what in fact it was supposed to do, but the replies were equally vague. In particular, the provision calling for "maximum feasible participation" of the poor was utterly ignored. Lillian Rubin, in an abstract concerning the subject, states that from the time of the antipoverty message in March to the enactment of the legislation in August, "no public discussion of the participation clause took place." Robert F. Kennedy was the only administration witness even to touch on the subject. In a statement prepared by Hackett, he declared, speaking of the existing social welfare structure:

They plan programs for the poor, not with them. Part of the sense of helplessness and futility comes from the feeling of powerlessness to affect the operations of these organizations. The community action programs must basically change these organizations by building into the program real representation for the poor. This bill calls for "maximum feasible participation of the residents." This means the involvement of the poor in planning and implementing programs: giving them a real voice in their institutions.

But no Congressman followed up on his statement.

This should not in itself be surprising. Kennedy was still, at this point, in a dazed, remote condition following the assassination. It was not likely anyone would press. But, Rubin records, "The Congressional debates are equally devoid of discussion about maximum feasible participation."[6] The administration was not calling attention to the point, and no one else noticed it. This was not a matter of Congressional quiescence. The issue of whether parochial schools would receive Federal aid under the proposed act became a matter of intense discussion. It was simply that no one in authority at either end of Pennsylvania Avenue regarded the participation clause as noteworthy.

On the other hand, in three separate actions Congress made it clear to anyone who wished to take note that it did not expect the antipoverty program to be a disruptive influence. First, in a meeting in the Speaker's Office on August 8th, members of the North Carolina delegation demanded as a price of their support a pledge that Yarmolinsky, who as the Assistant to the Secretary of Defense had energetically sought to uphold the constitutional rights of Negro servicemen in Southern states and was known for his generally liberal and progressive views, would have nothing to do with the administration of the antipoverty program. Shriver made a quick call to the White House. Yarmolinsky was sacrificed without ceremony or ado. The most effulgent promises of future preferment were made this dedicated man, who, weeks earlier, half-dead on an operating table after an automobile accident, had regained consciousness asking for details of the day's work on the antipoverty program. None were kept.

Secondly, a loyalty oath sponsored by the ineffable John Bell Williams of Mississippi was incorporated. Finally, the comprehensive planning provisions of Title II were in effect stricken.

In the final version of the administration bill a fourth clause was added to Sec. 202(a), which defined a "community action program." It was declared to be, along with the first three conditions, one

> (4) which is conducted, administered, or coordinated by a public or private nonprofit agency . . . which is broadly representative of the community.

The clause related to the Bureau of the Budget's persistent quest for something like comprehensive planning and coordination. The White House memorandum of January 21 had insisted that poverty could only be overcome if "all" public and private agencies worked together. The Senate amended this to provide for "maximum feasible participation of public agencies and private nonprofit organizations primarily concerned with the community's problems of poverty." This version was contained in S. 2642 which passed the Senate. In the House, however, the language was struck by an amendment from Congresswoman Green, who noted that the administration language had been left out of the bill reported from the Committee on Education and Labor as "the committee had no intention of having any comprehensive community-wide program as a prerequisite to granting Federal assistance."[7]

The final act provided simply:

> (4) which is conducted, administered, or coordinated by a public or private nonprofit agency (other than a political party), or a combination thereof.

The House Committee report on the bill, dated June 3, was even more explicit:[8]

> The committee anticipates that the Office of Economic Opportunity will encourage the development of community action programs which would carry out a multifaceted coordinated attack on the interrelated causes of poverty. It is not, however, the intention of the committee that the development of such a comprehensive community wide plan be a prerequisite to the extension of financial assistance to a public or private nonprofit agency for the development or execution of a program which gives promise of progress toward elimination of a cause or causes of poverty through developing employment opportunities, improving human performance, motivation, and productivity or bettering conditions under which people live, learn, and work.

My notes of the time report a day long meeting between Shriver and the Committee on May 7th at which this was agreed I wrote:

> Title II has been changed to cut back the requirements for a Comprehensive Community Action Plan—leaving it more flexible, and perhaps less efficacious, as well as a distinct burden on the Administrator who is given more discretion than is probably good for his peace of mind.

The move was primarily associated with Rep. Edith Green, whose impatience with academic Big Think in the President's Committee on Juvenile Delinquency and Youth Crime was already on record. Congress, or this element in it, wanted action without too much forethought, preparation, planning, negotiating, agreeing, staging. That is what it got.

If community action had been somewhat lost sight of within the administration, and never at all confronted as a significant issue by the Congress, it was still very much on the personal and political agenda of its original sponsors. As well it might have been. The first year appropriation for the antipoverty program, nearly $1 billion in theory, was in truth largely made up on sums already allocated to departmental legislative requests and subsequently subsumed under the heading of antipoverty funds, as the draft legislation itself was incorporated in the antipoverty bill. It was Title II that got the lion's share, $340 million, of the $500 million in "new" money originally set aside by the Bureau of the Budget for the antipoverty effort. For FY 1966, the amount was almost doubled. The professional reformers were doing very well indeed. Marris and Rein observe: "After four years of doubtful achievement, many frustrations, and a few precarious triumphs, the endeavour was rewarded by a fifty-fold increase in its funds."[9]

Here a quality of social scientists, as against social science, is involved. Excepting Ohlin and a few like him, the individuals taking part in these events were reformers first, professionals second. Their method was that of objective analysis of social systems, but their motive was a passionate desire for social change. Persons such as Cloward grew steadily more radical in their demands for the transformation of American society. The initial desire to facilitate entry into that system by outsiders (one section of the MFY prospectus was entitled "Expanding Opportunities for Conformity") was supplanted by a near detestation of the system itself. Many of the reformers of the 1950's came in the 1960's to associate themselves with James Baldwin's then-current taunt: who would wish to be integrated into a burning house? Something of this process had occurred with the delinquency program, where the necessity and desire to show some results repeatedly subverted the effort to test a social hypothesis. "The logic of scientific problem solving," Marris and Rein record, "collapsed in piecemeal pragmatism."[10]

Something of this same process now took hold within the cohorts Shriver now assembled to plan the

implementation of the antipoverty program once it
was enacted. (They were to hit the ground running.
A fair judgment of subsequent events must take account of the sense of drama and urgency which suffused the atmosphere of Washington at this time, and
which was perhaps enhanced by Shriver's own ebul-
lient, tireless, determined leadership.) With the submission of the legislation in March, Shriver's task
force quickly grew into a full-scale staging operation.
The original members, save Yarmolinsky and for a
period Sundquist, returned to their departments. New
men of lower rank succeeded them. Their loyalties
were wholly to the new program. This now burgeoning
organization included many of the most forceful and
committed advocates of community action that had
originally gathered around Hackett and the PCJD—
Richard Boone, Sanford Kravitz, Frederick O'R. Hayes
—and others such as Harold Horowitz of HEW and
Erich Tolmach of Labor who had become involved with
the concept. This group was assembled as an Urban
Areas Task Force to draw up guidelines for the CAP's
that were to swing into action the moment the legis
lation was signed. (In the event, the President, wisely,
held the program in abeyance until the November elections were passed.) Jack Conway, a former United
Automobile Workers official, who had become Walter
Reuther's principal representative in the hierarchy of
of the AFL-CIO headquarters in Washington, came
aboard as co-chairman of this group.

At this point two of the moves taken in the Congress to prevent the "radicalization" of the antipoverty
program had just the opposite effect. By eliminating
the requirement, or expectation, of comprehensive
planning and the creation of "broadly representative"
organizations, Congress left the antipoverty warriors
(as they came to be known) free to go into action

immediately. It also left them free in reality to turn over the local CAP to whomsoever they wished. Gone was Boone's estimate of February 3 that "one year plus" would be required to get a CAP into operation. Gone was Ylvisaker's vision of an assemblage of the power structure as a prerequisite, as indeed the purpose, of the CAP. Had Yarmolinsky stayed on in charge of the planning of the program and then become Deputy Director, it can be assumed that these unexpected liberties would have been exercised with a measure of restraint. A careful and seasoned man, accustomed to the inhibitions imposed by power, and fiercely protective of the Presidency, he would have been at once more responsive to the wishes of Congress and more concerned with the "respectability" of the program. But Congress had blocked Yarmolinsky's appointment. Instead, the job went to Conway, who had none of these inhibitions or necessary concerns, and was moreover, brought into the operation in the first instance to plan the community action component. An immensely competent man, and for all his rank-and-file exterior, as much an ADA intellectual as anything else, Conway had no particular intention of making trouble for the Johnson administration, but his first concern was in another direction. Where the President hoped to help the poor, Conway wished to arouse them. That in a sense was his profession. He was a labor organizer on the militant wing of the labor movement. Where the first reaction to the appointment of the Shriver task force among George Meany's aides had been alarm that the "leftist"—that is, anti-labor-establishment—writer, Paul Jacobs seemed to be being consulted, the attitude of the CIO representatives was much more responsive to such advocates of opening the labor movement to the poor and recapturing the radical passions of the 1930's. Conway was fully in favor of shaking things up.

For this purpose the all-but-forgotten term "maximum feasible participation" was decisive. In an interview Conway later stated that his concern "was to structure community action programs so that they would have an immediate and irreversible impact on the communities."[11] To this end, as Blumenthal shows, the Conway group through the spring and summer of 1964 gradually expanded its notion of how much, at what stage, and for what purpose the poor were to be involved with the community action programs. The logic of the matter took them all the way. In the end they concluded that it would be as much as possible, at all stages, and for every purpose. The *Community Action Program Guide* puts the matter succinctly at the outset:[12]

A vital feature of every community action program is the involvement of the poor themselves—the residents of the areas and members of the groups to be served—in planning, policymaking, and operation of the program.

A tripartite arrangement was envisaged—Conway referred to it as a "three-legged stool"—between established agencies, leadership groups ("labor, business, religious, and minority groups"), and representatives of the local poor. But the heart of the matter was the "mobilization" of the poor themselves. "The requirement of resident participation," the *Guide* continues, "applies to all stages of a community action program, from its inception on." Participation must be "meaningful" and "effective." It should be brought about by "traditional democratic approaches and techniques such as group forums and discussions, nominations, and balloting." It should be stimulated by "grass-roots involvement" committees; by "block elections, petitions and referendums"; by "newsletters to neighborhood leaders and potential leaders"; by "promotional techniques, including use of films, literature, and mobile units operating from information centers." Further, residents should be given "meaningful opportunities . . . either as individuals or in groups, to protest or to propose additions to or changes in the ways in which a community action program is being planned or undertaken." As Blumenthal concludes, "These members of the Task Force clearly envisioned the creation of new institutions, representing the demands of the poor."[13]

Not much is to be achieved by asking whether the Conway group exceeded its instructions. It had no instructions. What it had was a seeming opportunity to set in motion forces for social change that its members desired to see occur. It seized the opportunity. Nonetheless, two comments must be made.

First, the Conway group gave to the community action programs of the poverty program a structure that neither those who drafted it, those who sponsored it, nor those who enacted it ever in any way intended. To do this was a risk—worth taking from a certain point of view, but a risk withal.

Second, the forces that the Conway group sought to set in motion would operate primarily within the Negro slums of the nation's large cities. This was foreseeable, and was indeed a primary expectation of the Conway group. However, the various planning groups were made up exclusively of middle-class whites. At no time did any Negro have any role of any consequence in the drafting of the poverty program. Nor did any Negro have any role of any consequence in the drafting of the CAP guidelines. Yet it was the Negro community that was to be primarily affected. Whether Negro involvement—participation—in *this* planning process would have produced the same formula cannot be said. But it is clear to the degree that risks were involved, whites were taking them for blacks.

All this might have mattered less, save for an event that occurred before the antipoverty program was sent to Congress. As the Shriver task force proceeded with its work in January and February, the case for a massive employment program grew steadily stronger, not least out of a desire to add something distinctive to what was otherwise only a collection of other people's proposals. Shriver was persuaded. On February 18 he presented the task force's proposals to a meeting of the cabinet. Among them was a proposed 5-cent tax on cigarettes expected to yield $1.25 billion per year to be earmarked for employment programs for the adult poor. Secretary of Labor Wirtz spoke in favor of the idea; the rest of the cabinet was silent. But the President dismissed it immediately. He was seeking that year to cut taxes, not to raise them. The matter was concluded, and unlike most, never made its way into the newspapers.[14]

Had Shriver's employment proposal succeeded, the character of the antipoverty program would have changed. In the first place, it would have dwarfed the other items, but more importantly, it would have given an unavoidably "conservative" cast to the entire undertaking. The program leadership would of necessity have found itself emphasizing the prudent, frugal, constructive nature of the work being done by deserving men receiving, at most, a modest day's pay for a hard day's work. The energies and attention of the administration would have been turned to the vital task of reforming and restructuring the job market. In a word, an "employment strategy" would have become central to the war on poverty. But this did not happen.

Further, two of the three adolescent employment programs of Title I—the Neighborhood Youth Corps and the Work Study program—were immediately turned over to other departments, their original sponsors. This left OEO with the Job Corps and Community Action. The tendency of both was to oversell and underperform. Shriver gave himself to this process with a singular lack of reflection. In short order he was describing the community action program as "the business corporation of the new social revolution." An absurd proposition, but an old maxim: when you can't get reform you get revolution—sometimes.

*NOTES*

1. Marris and Rein, *op. cit.*, p. 135.
2. *Ibid.*, p. 209.
3. See also John E. Moore, "Delinquency: Presidential, Congressional and Juvenile," in *Cases in Urban Legislation* (Washington: Brookings Institution, 1967).
4. This is my recollection. I have no notes of the occasion. However, it is confirmed by Yarmolinsky's notes and by William Capron in an interview, November 23, 1966, with Richard Blumenthal.
5. Richard Blumenthal, "Community Action: The Origins of a Government Program," Senior Thesis, Harvard College, 1967, Chapter V.
6. Lillian Rubin, "Maximum Feasible Participation, The Origins, Implications, and Present Status," *Poverty and Human Resources Abstracts* (November-December, 1967). Kennedy's statement will be found in House Committee on Education and Labor, Hearings on the Economic Opportunity Act of 1964, 88th Congress, 2nd Session, 1964, pp. 207–212, 301–339.
7. *U.S. Congressional Record*, August 7, 1964, p. 17, 997.
8. 88th Congress, Second Session, House of Representatives, Report No. 1458, Economic Opportunity Act of 1964, p. 11.
9. Marris and Rein, *op. cit.*, p. 208.
10. *Ibid.*, p. 214.

11. Blumenthal, *op. cit.*, p. 122.

12. Office of Economic Opportunity, *Community Action Program Guide,* Washington, D.C., October 1965.

13. Blumenthal, *op. cit.*, p. 125.

14. Daniel P. Moynihan, "The Poor Professors," in *On Understanding Poverty: Perspectives from the Social Sciences,* edited by Daniel P. Moynihan. Vol. I of a compilation of essays written for the American Academy of Arts and Sciences' Seminar on Poverty. (New York: Basic Books, to be published in 1969.) See also Adam Yarmolinsky, "The Beginnings of OEO," in *On Fighting Poverty: Perspectives from Experience,* edited by James Sundquist, Vol. II of the American Academy of Arts and Sciences.

# CHAPTER SIX

# "MOBILIZATION
# FOR
# YOUTH LOST"

On August 16, 1964, four days before the Economic
Opportunity Act was signed, the *New York Daily News*
declared that Mobilization For Youth had become in-
fested with subversives, or as the phrase became,
"Commies and Commie sympathizers." This ambitious
and adventurous undertaking, which had provided the
model for much of the community action program of
the war on poverty was now also to anticipate the
urban furor soon to break out across the nation.

*The Daily News:* The nation's largest newspaper.
The hands-down favorite reading matter of the poor
people of New York City. In style, in attitude, in politics, the opposite of just about everything represented
by MFY. Few seem to know who runs the *News;* apparently it largely runs itself. It is enormously profitable

and its executives reputedly pay themselves accordingly. It is well written and well edited; it is lively, alert, and when it chooses to be, is in ways the most informative paper in New York on the subject of City and State politics. One source of its journalistic strength is that the people read the *News:* politicians know it and wish their views recorded in it. If it were apolitical, or simply conservative, it would be in ways an admirable affair, but it is neither of those things: its politics are consistently and nastily illiberal, anti-intellectual, superpatriotic, and at times savagely anti-communist. The irony of this, of course, and the fact that continually trips up liberal, intellectual middle-class reformers, is that the *News* is in ways merely a caricature of the worst (though not the dominant) tendencies of the working and lower-class masses of the City who follow it so faithfully. In a certain sense, the reactionary qualities of the *News* reflect a kind of populism gone sour, a phenomenon not dissimilar to that which occurred in the South. Its tone is rather that of the decent enough Tammany politician displaced—and *disgraced*—by middle-class reformers. As it is said of Ireland that it missed the Protestant reformation and the industrial revolution, it may be said of the *Daily News* that it has been completely untouched by two of the dominant influences in New York life—the tradition of social responsibility among the Protestant élite, and the tradition of social radicalism among the Jewish middle class. Mobilization For Youth, with Winslow Carlton as its chairman and the Columbia School of Social Work as its driving force, represented a singularly avowed and, as it turned out, painfully exposed merger of both those traditions. Dispatching a *Daily News* reporter to check up on MFY was sending a goat to the cabbage patch.

In a pattern that was to be reproduced over and

again elsewhere, it was not the employment or education programs of MFY that drew the *News* fire; it was community action. It was here, the charge went, that radicals had moved in and begun their heinous work of disrupting the social order. It will be remembered that New York had been shaken by Negro rioting in 1963, the first such incident in a sequence that was to shake the nation. A favorite charge of the *News,* almost certainly untrue, is that MFY reproduction equipment was used to print a poster with a picture of the police officer whose shooting of a Negro youth presumedly helped trigger the Harlem riot. "Wanted for Murder," was the caption, "Gilligan the Cop." Thus the *News* also anticipated, and set a pattern of sorts, for white apprehension and suspicion that Negro riots were planned disturbances and that Marxist radicals were behind them.

Certain of the *Daily News* charges are of a kind that can never be fully answered, but the issue of Communist infiltration can be. Of some three hundred MFY employees at this period, it appears that two may at that time have been members of the Communist Party, and two were similarly likely to have been members of the Socialist Workers Party. There was some suggestion of past Communist Party membership with respect to nineteen other employees. Altogether there was some "derogatory information," to use the FBI term for assertions that may or may not turn out to be true on further enquiry, on about thirty-two employees. This information was assembled by the FBI for the Attorney General shortly after the *News* charges were made public. Given that the Attorney General was chairman of the Presidential committee that was helping to fund MFY, it may be assumed that the enquiry was done with care, and on this basis, then, it can be stated that the *News* charge of large scale "Commie" infiltration was false.

If the implication was that the Communist Party had made or was making an effort to influence or direct MFY activity, it may be said on the basis of the evidence that this charge also was false. The Federal government is not at a loss to determine the answers to such questions: it merely enquires of its informers. A memorandum of August 31, 1964, from the Attorney General to a White House official put the matter with customary delicacy: "material received from sources in a position to report on the day-to-day activity of Communist Party National and State headquarters, fails to reveal any effort by the Communist Party to dominate, control or infiltrate MFY."

But such evidence has little to do with such controversy. The more relevant fact, or set of facts, is that the community organizing efforts of MFY did give rise, both within the staff and the neighborhood, to attitudes and actions distinctly reminiscent of Marxist agitation of earlier days, and could readily be misrepresented as just that. The reaction among "ritualistic liberals," as one member of the non-Communist left working on the Lower East Side at this time described them, would be, and was to demand, a clean bill of health for the organization, and to do so with not a little righteous indignation. But public officials were just as likely to be fearful that there might just be something to the charges—and in the case of MFY there was *something*—to panic and to act badly. To some degree this did happen in New York. (It will be recalled, that at this time a vengeful right-wing conservatism seemed to be taking over the Republican Party. The prospect that "Chinese" communists—such was the rumor—might turn up on quasi-public payrolls organizing the masses of the Lower East Side was not altogether reassuring.) Similar reactions were to occur elsewhere. It would seem to be a frequent sequence in the progress of community action.

As in the Federal antipoverty program, much the greatest portion of the MFY budget was devoted to programs in the World of Work, the World of Education, and its other services of individuals and groups. In its second year of operation, the Community Program received only $272,000. On the other hand, from the outset this program received almost all the publicity, and just as importantly it seems to have been the activity that most exhilarated the middle class professionals working at MFY. (One MFY official told a reporter that the 300-man staff spent 80 to 90 per cent of its energies "organizing the unaffiliated—the lower fifth of the economic ladder . . . who will overturn the status quo" in the neighborhood.[1]

This activity, formally titled "Organizing the Unaffiliated" was very much the prototype of the community action programs of the OEO. As with all of MFY's programs it was derived, step by step, from general to specific hypotheses, each step accompanied by citations from the work of major sociologists: Eleanor Maccoby on "Community Integration and the Social Control of Delinquency,"[2] Morris Axelrod on "Urban Structure and Social Participation,"[3] W. G. Mather on "Income and Social Participation,"[4] Peter Rossi on *Why Families Move*.[5] The general hypothesis was direct enough:[6]

Participation by adults in decision-making about matters that affect their interests increases their sense of identification with the community and the larger social order. People who identify with their neighborhood and share common values are more likely to try to control juvenile misbehavior. A well-integrated community can provide learning experiences for adults which enable them to serve as more adequate models and interpreters of community life for the young. In short, there is an inverse relation between community integration and the rates of juvenile misbehavior.

Four barriers to such integration were identified: lower class families moved a great deal; community activities were typically staffed by middle-class personnel; the self-defeating attitudes of the lower class made them feel nothing could be accomplished; and, finally, "intergroup tensions" kept the community fragmented. Little could be done about the first difficulty, but tactics were quickly devised for the remaining three: the "indigenous disadvantaged" would be employed by MFY to help organize and stimulate the community; "issues" would be chosen that were at once highly visible and gave promise of immediate payoff; and finally, the groups would be organized along racial and ethnic lines. MFY decided to concentrate almost its entire attention on the Negroes and Puerto Ricans of the neighborhood.

Out of this orderly, and conservative formulation— this was, after all, nothing more than an effort to give grown ups in the neighborhood roles that would encourage them to teach their kids to behave — came a  series of events that many in the larger world, especially the political world, was to view as dangerous and disorderly conduct. The MFY Prospectus had stated, accurately enough, that "The task of developing a theory of action which is consistent with the theory of causation is, of course, immense."[7] As it turned out, however, an even greater if unexpected difficulty was that of retaining over time the same concept of causation and the same object of action. MFY began with the understanding that the problem of the poor was anomie; in short order anomie was replaced by "powerlessness" as the fundamental disorder. It started out to create cooperative arrangements that would open the neighborhood opportunity structure to deviant or potentially deviant youths; in short order the opportunity structure was being defined as a power structure, and itself accused of deviance in the largest social sense of good and bad behavior. Rhetorically at all events, reform inched towards revolution. Right or wrong, MFY did not very long remain the carefully calibrated social experiment it had set out to be.

The shift from anomie to powerlessness would seem in part related to the problem of size. In a city of eight million, Mobilization for Youth represented an area of 100,000 persons and was actively concerned with only a third of these. Almost all of the principal "institutions" that affected the residents of the Lower East Side—the school system, the labor market, the housing, the police force—were at least city-wide in their organization and scope, and most had state and national ties. A neighborhood group would sense little leverage in such situations.

The "problem" of powerlessness must surely also have been compounded by the erosion of community-based political power, a change especially to be noted in Manhattan where for so long local political organizations, coalescing in Tammany Hall, had wielded highly visible, even notorious power. Fifty years of municipal reform had just about put an end to that in New York. Not the least ironic of MFY's experience is that much of the impulse to do something about the feeling of powerlessness among the lower-class ethnic minorities of the city came from much the same group that in previous decades had systematically stripped minorities of the very considerable power they had had, and did so in the name of their own good. What more conclusive evidence of evil could be adduced against a local political leader during the 1950's, the more so if he were Italian, say, and had taken to wearing expensive clothes, than to charge that he was a "Boss,"—that is, that he had power! Nothing if not self-aware, the MFY Prospectus provided a theory of the urban political machine as well, suggesting in effect that the Italians and Irish had taken Tammany with them, into the lower middle class and would no longer allow it to perform its traditional functions. There was something in this, but the larger fact is that those functions had for the most part been taken out of the political sector and consigned to bureaucracies—the very bureaucracies whose middle-class rigidity and putative disdain for the poor had been responsible for so much of the thinking behind community action! Further, uniformity and consistency, the treatment of like cases alike, is the essence of the bureaucratic method and a central demand of the good government reformers in the campaign against the "favoritism" so characteristic of the working-class style in politics. With the best will in the world, the City departments could not set up special rules for a few square blocks on the Lower East Side. And those few square blocks hardly had the power to force the rules to be changed for the entire city, where in any event their views were not necessarily shared.

During this period, Kenneth B. Clark was preparing the large study from which the community action agency of Harlem, HARYOU-ACT was shaped. Where MFY had been theory-oriented, Clark's study rested largely on field research: What did the youth of Harlem feel? What did they need? It was in ways even a more impressive piece of work than its downtown counterpart, and came to essentially the same conclusions as did MFY. It was titled: "Youth in the Ghetto: A Study in the Consequences of Powerlessness." Yet by traditional New York standards there was no reason for Harlem to feel powerless. Negroes at this time were in complete control of their local political organizations: Harlem had powerful representatives at the City, State, and national levels of government. Yet somehow the power of such representatives to effect local events had diminished. Thus one of the galling facts of life in Harlem was the treasure that poured out of the community daily in consequence of the gambling and narcotics traffic operated illegally by whites. In an earlier age the police would have regulated this commerce and the political machine would have regulated the police. But, at about this time, when Congressman Adam Clayton Powell, no doubt other concerns in mind, demanded that a Negro police captain be assigned to Harlem, the Irish Commissioner, not perhaps without a twinge of regret, informed the Congressman that Tammany district leaders (which Powell also was) no longer appointed police captains in New York. Bureaucracy had taken over, the next man on the list would be appointed, etc., etc. As the MFY Prospectus had stated, "the machine humanized and personalized its services. It provided help and favors rather than justice and assistance."[8] Bureaucracies may not do this—must not.

It would appear that these municipal facts of life had important consequences on the tactics of Mobilization's effort to organize the unaffiliated. Inasmuch as so little in the way of institutional change could be accomplished in the neighborhood, it became necessary to escalate the level at which demands were made to that of the City Hall, at very least, where changes in bureaucratic institutions could be affected. This meant expanding the scope of demands from local to citywide propositions. Just possibly the middle-class reformers felt more at home at such levels—their turf

—but conditions also encouraged what might have been a predisposition.

The immediate consequence of this was an escalation in rhetoric. More and more George Brager, director of MFY's Action Programs was talking about the "powerlessness" of the poor *with respect to city government.* A program that had begun as a promising device for helping to resolve the private difficulties of young persons, which in the aggregate were creating a social problem, a device the city government was more than willing to support and encourage, began of a sudden to pose a challenge to that very government. And here the personal qualities of the middle-class professional reformers, elite academics and intellectuals for the most part, contributed not a little to the mounting tension. For if capable of the deepest empathy, the purest Christian compassion for the poor, too frequently they had nothing but contempt for the working class, lower-middle-class bureaucratic and political cadres that ran the city. The belief that suffering purifies and that security corrupts is deep in Western culture, and nowhere so manifest as among young educated Americans coming of age in the 1950's, having experienced all their lives an absolute minimum of suffering and an absolute maximum of security. One dares to detect a measure of glee, almost, as the MFY theorists turned on City Hall, capitalism, racism, America itself. There is to be seen in their *MF* writings, as Leonard Chazen notes, a steady "progression from a politically neutral concern with organizing the slums to a fully engaged animus for the city 'Establishment.'"[9] This is *not* to be explained in terms of the particular social and political setting in which MFY was trying to function. At this time a radical, middle class stirring was beginning to be felt throughout the nation. "Expanding Opportunities for Conformity" may have expressed the spirit of the 1950's on the Columbia campus: it was not the "thing" for the 1960's. It is difficult to resist the impression that the MFY principles were as much affected by changing fashions in ideas, as by any pragmatic response to a particular set of circumstances.

Cloward in particular underwent a process of radicalization. Chazen describes a 1965 article by him as "bearing all the bitterness of an SDS pamphlet on urban politics." At once a major actor and a highly representative one, a full understanding of the progress of the idea of community action in the 1960's must await an explanation of the steps by which men such as he progressed from social work in a military prison to the most intransigent defiance of the social system itself. Perhaps as they learned more about the system, they became more opposed to it. Perhaps as the system proved sluggish in response to their initiatives, they grew more determined to impose their will. But for certain, men such as Cloward moved fairly rapidly from the effort to integrate the poor into the system to an effort to use the poor to bring down the whole rotten structure. In the late 1960's Cloward turned to the organization of welfare mothers with the avowed intent of putting so many families on welfare that the fiscal structure of State and local government would collapse. His plans went from cooperating with City Hall, to defying it, to taking it over. Writing with a colleague in *The Nation* in 1967 on the subject of "Corporate Imperialism for the Poor," his term for the growing interest of business corporations at this time in investing in the "ghetto," he explained the development in conventional, if vulgar, Marxist terms:[10]

First, corporate enterprise no longer has major stakes in domestic racism. Historically, racism helped to perpetuate a caste system that produced a surplus of cheap black labor.

That surplus was used against white workers, chiefly to undermine wage levels; more directly, blacks were hired as scabs and goons to impede efforts by whites to unionize.

He warned against the poor accepting the embrace of the capitalists, especially in conjunction with increased Federal activities that would withdraw power from local government. He then asked instead that Federal funds go directly to city government, as they have done in the past through grants-in-aid, so that "black municipal leaders could convert these funds into jobs, services and facilities required not only to improve economic conditions but to consolidate a black electorate as well."[11] Don't fight City Hall: capture it. But this was 1967. In 1963 and 1964, New York City Hall municipal government was increasingly defined by MFY as the enemy.

The MFY internal notes from the period are filled with the minutiae and the exhilaration of combat. Problem: "No matter how we disguise it, irrespective of letterhead and who signs the letters, telegrams, etc., City agencies quickly begin to realize which letters and which buildings come to them from Mobilization for Youth." Solution: "Transform *every* housing program currently sponsored by MFY into tenant membership organizations. There need be no exceptions." Future battles were planned. The Housing Committee would become a "rent strike coordinating committee." "We are drawing together and staffing a committee which will coordinate all direct action campaigns in a militant manner. . . . This is an organization of organizations, and contains the kind of fighting, sophisticated politicized organizations who are just itching to play out the 'Jesse Gray' role and 'bring to the Lower East Side what Harlem has begun.' . . . Only massive rent strikes are effective in obtaining publicity, embarrassing the establishment, etc."[12]

It must be kept in mind that Mobilization for Youth was in every sense a creature of that very establishment: Columbia University, the Ford Foundation, the Mayor of New York, the President of the United States. Now it was setting out to embarrass it. That had not been the plan, but that was how it was working out. In Robert F. Wagner they found an especially vulnerable target, an immensely decent man, increasingly worn down by the demands of what was now his third term as Mayor, yet incapable of truly vengeful retaliation, trying only to keep the city running. The trade unions had long ago learned to strike friends first, and MFY understood this about Wagner. But he *was* human. Herbert Krosney writes: [13]

Mobilization gave counsel to and worked with downtown CORE. This group later dumped dead rats on Mayor Wagner's doorstep, a gesture which, however vivid, was not calculated to gain the Mayor's sympathy.

A second general difficulty which MFY soon encountered, and which would seem to be an endemic risk of community action, involved the issue of ethnic antagonism. In seeking to enlarge the community, to bring in outsiders, they soon found themselves fractionating it. When class conflict is induced in an American urban community, it would seem to have a natural tendency to assert itself in terms of ethnic conflict as well. At the outset MFY made the decision to organize specifically Puerto Rican and Negro groups and to bring them into battle with the establishment. Plans specified the ethnicity of employees: "Henry Street Tenants' Council; *Area*–Madison to East Broadway, Montgomery to Pike; *Staff*–Negro community worker to be hired, plus Pedro—." (Such practices were of course to be forbidden by the Civil Rights Act of 1964!)

In one of its first tests, this technique backfired.

An organization of Puerto Rican mothers, with the acronym MOM, was put together for the purpose of a "conflict confrontation" with the principal of the local P.S. 140, Irving Rosenbloom. The principal was accused of bigotry and it was demanded that he be fired. The confrontation was noisy, disorderly, and something ominously close to antisemitism made its appearance. Twenty-six public school principals in the area responded with a telegram to Mayor Wagner demanding instead that Brager, head of the MFY action program, be fired. His community workers, the telegram stated,[14]

[were] becoming full-time paid agitators and organizers for extremist groups. This constitutes an abuse of the noble purpose for which great sums of federal and municipal money were originally appropriated. This movement has been subverted from its original plan to war against delinquency into a war against individual schools and their leaders, to what purpose we cannot at the present time divine.

Now the issue arose as to just how representative the mothers' group was. James McNamara, a member of the local school board and the local leader of the Liberal Party, defended Rosenbloom as a good man, and attacked MOM as a "phantom organization led by MFY staff members." The letter to the superintendent of schools demanding Rosenbloom's resignation contained only twenty valid signatures of 200—"the rest were forgeries." The problem, said McNamara, "stems from the theory that you must get the lower fifth excited and that they must fight the power structure." If that was the problem, it was also the avowed intention of MFY at this point. Shortly after the incident at P.S. 140, the first civil rights boycott of the New York schools occurred. Whether or not there was a valid connection, there were those willing to perceive one.

The Negro Action Group (NAG) took on an even more ominous turn. Although this was a time when relations between Negro militants and white liberals were at their most cordial and effective state, the deliberate effort to bring about conflict between a Negro lower-class group and the city establishment displayed a potential for divisiveness that was to become reality all too soon. NAG was intended to be an outrageous organization, and from all reports it was. Although MFY was to deny the charge when it was made by the *News*, Jesse Gray, the rent strike organizer who had acquired a reputation during the 1963 Harlem riot, was indeed involved with MFY's efforts to start rent strikes on the Lower East Side. He provided an important model for action, and perhaps also a vocabulary that could only inflame relations with whites.[15] An activist in downtown CORE insisted to the journalist Jack Newfield that NAG was "nationalistic and anti-Semitic" and refused to cooperate with CORE, which was vigorously interracial at that time. "This is an inevitable consequence," he continued, "of a strategy that intentionally pits Negroes and Puerto Ricans against a predominantly Jewish establishment."[16] This development was to become even more pronounced later on. Thus in the dispute at I.S. 201 in East Harlem in the winter of 1966–67 in which local residents, much supported by the local community action agency (MEND) demanded the ouster of principal Stanley R. Lisser, the *New York Times* reported that "the street agitation . . . was flagrantly anti-white and anti-Semitic." In 1968 when the issue of community control of the Ocean Hill-Brownsville school district—another Ford Foundation experimental project—was raging, one leaflet took the matter to considerable lengths, declaring:

If African-American History and Culture is to be taught to our Black Children it Must be Done by African-Americans Who Identify With and Who Understand the Problem. It is Impossible For the Middle East Murderers of Colored People to Possibly Bring To This Important Task The Insight, The Concern, The Exposing of the Truth that is a *Must* If The Years of Brainwashing And Self-Hatred That Has Been Taught To Our Black Children By These Blood-sucking Exploiters and Murderers Is To Be Overcome. The Idea Behind This Program Is Beautiful, But When The Money Changers Heard About It They Took Over, As Is Their Custom In the Black Community. If African American History and Culture Is important To Our Children [to] Raise Their Esteem Of Themselves, They Are [sic] The Only Persons Who Can Do The Job Are African-American Brothers and Sisters, And Not the So-Called Liberal Jewish Friend. We know From His Tricksy, Deceitful Maneuvers That He is Really Our Enemy and *He* is Responsible For the Serious Educational Retardation of Our Black Children.

Pretty sentiments, to which there were Jews capable of responding in kind. Charles E. Silberman, the distinguished author of *Crisis in Black and White,* spotted the trend and in May 1968 demanded of a meeting sponsored by the American Jewish Committee that it "face up to the raw, rank, anti-Negro prejudice that is within our own midst. We talk—endlessly—about Negro Anti-Semitism; we rarely talk about—let alone try to deal with—the Jewish Anti-Negroism that is in our midst and that is growing very rapidly."[17] Demanding power for a black community rather quickly became a demand for black power. This may have been therapeutic for those involved, but the reaction elsewhere, as Vice President Humphrey later declared in an interview arranged by the American Jewish Community, was "consternation and confusion."[18]

MFY was not responsible for the rise of Negro extremism or black nationalism. It was simply there when the storm broke, and it was useful as a vehicle in its part of the City. It is to the credit of those who conceived and began the program that while the nation generally was either unaware of the mounting fury within the Negro community, or at best indifferent to it, MFY leaders had already set out to do something about it. It is part of the irony that suffuses the MFY experience that the institutions they helped establish were put to uses (miniscule and of no substantive consequence on the Lower East Side, but important in terms of the idea) that were just the opposite of what they had envisaged. Their fondest hope was to enable the slum youth they served to enter the larger society, to conform to its standards, and to succeed by them. Alas, by the time the program was underway the issue had already been raised by Negro writers such as James Baldwin as to whether the standards of the white community were worth conforming to. "Subsequent classes of black students," a Negro youth at Columbia was to declare some years later, "will not only reject the white man's hang-ups, but will also reject the mediocre goals this institution says they ought to aspire to: they will absolutely refuse the white man's benevolent offer of a '32nd vice niggership' at General Motors."[19] Seen from the perspective of other groups, this was rather a conventional statement for a certain type of New York student, but no law provides that Negroes shall follow in the footsteps of those who preceded them in the great city, and certainly there were many who at this point intended nothing of the sort. The extreme left was reasserting its influence, its aim, as Max Lerner writes, "to radicalize the Negro and convert him into the cutting edge that will divide America and throw it into the kind of chaos out of which revolutionary situations are made."[20] This was hardly the intent of MFY, but a whiff of this notion drifted uptown from East Second Street. Rent strikes? School boycotts? Voter registration drives? Mass demonstrations? "What this has to do with curbing juvenile delinquency," declared the *New York Herald Tribune* "or why public funds should be used, is a cause for bafflement."[21]

If liberal Republican editorial writers were puzzled,

so might social reformers be. The logic of events was moving MFY ever closer to Saul Alinsky's famous formula for organizing the unorganized: "rub raw the sores of discontent."[22] If there is no discontent—that is to say, if apathetic resignation has effectively repressed incipient militancy—create hate objects and enable the individual in the mass to give expression to his justified anger. The problem for the MFY theorists, and in this one respect they must be faulted, is that as they got caught up in the thrill of battle, they quite failed to see the degree to which the strategy of induced conflict contradicted their own theory of anomie, or at least would in all probable reality lead to an increase rather than a decrease in anomic withdrawal. Durkheim saw society becoming a "dust of individuals" whose ties to one another were lost in the rationalist desiccation. Merton evolved this into a set of principles of social action which stressed the significance of frustration. Cloward and Ohlin applied the principles to the problem of delinquency. At this point, the temperament of the professional reformer once again enters the equation. The opportunity theory, although quite balanced in its assessment of individual as against social responsibility, can, like certain optical illusions, oscillate so that one moment one side appears dominant, while the next moment the mind's eye shifts and the dominance alternates. The social system frustrates the aspirations of the delinquent individual. True. Or at least hypothetically true. But also, the delinquent may have unreal aspirations so that he in effect frustrates himself. In the planning stages of the Ford Foundation community development program, Ohlin gave some prominence to this latter phenomenon. In a paper prepared for Ford in 1960 he wrote:[23]

The community development problem that I have in mind is the commonly observed inability of new migrants to provide their children with realistic expectations or access to opportunities for achieving their aspirations. This deficiency on the part of new migrants arises in large part from a state of alienation from urban culture. . . . For example, the diminishing vitality of the local political machine, with its autocratic and attentive political boss, eliminates an important interpretive link to the new world for migrants. . . . Under such conditions the adult migrants, lacking secure conceptions of the new cultural norms, induce in their children unrealistic expectations which are unrelated in any case to observable, relevant structures of opportunities by which these expectations may be achieved.

As the 1960's moved on, the problem of unrealistic expectations began to be compounded by a seeming depreciation of heretofore decent-enough jobs which the poor were now said to find unacceptable. (Said, to be sure, "by spokesmen.") In 1968, Paul Goodman publically puzzled over this:[24]

Sensitive minds . . . understand perfectly that just to get into the middle-class American mainstream is not humanly good enough; but then it is hard . . . to explain to poor people what, these days, would be humanly good enough. Consider the current social imputation of many jobs as "menial." When I was young, driving a bus or trailer-truck was manly, difficult, and responsible; now when there are many black drivers, it is ordinary. Construction work used to be skilled; but a black or Spanish bricklayer or mason tends to be considered unskilled. White road-workers in Vermont have a decent job; black road-workers with the same equipment have a menial job. Postman, a job requiring unusual tact and judgment has always been a dignified occupation; now that, like other Federal employment, it is open to many blacks, my guess is that it will be considered drab. . . . This social imputation of worth is made, of course, by both whites and blacks. . . . The question is why the blacks go along with the same imputation. . . . In this frame of mind, it is impossible to be free and independent.

As a matter of temperament, a fair proportion of professional reformers will reject—or repress—Ohlin's latter observation. The aspirations of the poor ought *not* to be unrealistic. Only a callous, corrupt society makes them unrealistic. Every child a brain surgeon. The story is told of Daniel O'Connell, the Irish popular leader of the early nineteenth century, who, approaching an old man working on the road one day, sent the laborer into a paroxysm of patriotic effusion. "Calm yourself, old man," said O'Connell. "Whether I win or lose, you will still be breaking rocks." Rejecting such realism as somehow immoral, MFY's leaders unavoidably turned to increasing demands on the power structure, in much the manner of the black power movement that was just then getting started. Repeatedly these demands were not met, or if they were, new and larger demands were put forth in order to maintain the dynamic of conflict and confrontation. Chazen offers the formula:[25]

$$\text{Frustration} = \text{Aspiration/Achievement}$$

If that is the case, would it not follow that increasing aspirations through community-wide conflict will also increase frustration when it is not accompanied by fairly rapid and tangible achievement? Hence an increase in anomie, and accordingly in deviant behavior. Is that in fact what happened to urban Negro society in the 1960's? The question is neither absurd nor unanswerable, although of course answers do not now exist.

At all events, before the social scientist associated with MFY could reasonably be expected to have reached any judgments on the effects of community agitation, their freedom of action was for practical purposes taken from them. The *Daily News* charges about Communist infiltration in MFY were picked up by conservative political leaders in New York and expanded to include the entire antipoverty program. In the City, a Queens Republican, Joseph Modugno, proposed that a City Council committee be established to keep an eye on all such activities: the HARYOU-ACT volume "Youth in the Ghetto," he declared, contains "radical sociological ideas, which might allow professional agitators to bring about an economic-social revolution in our city."[26]

The City government was considerably unnerved. The Federal antipoverty program was just then getting underway, as was the Goldwater-Johnson campaign. City officials explained in Washington that they were not the least impressed by the Communist charges, but that something had to be done to get control of the MFY community action program. The decision was made to do so, and in the event MFY—despite wide support and a full page *New York Times* advertisement —was powerless to defend itself.[27] Its money came from Washington and City Hall. In short order the head of the organization, James E. McCarthy, who had been accused of excessive use of entertainment funds, resigned, and MFY, which had had great independence of operations, was directed to conduct all future business—purchasing, contracting, hiring— through the regular City departments. Bertram Beck, the respected official of the National Association of Social Workers, was brought in as the new Executive Director of MFY, at $30,000 per year. Calm was restored. But the spirit seems somehow to have gone out of the undertaking. Outwardly unaffected, it had inwardly changed. David Hackett later put it to Herbert Krosney: "Mobilization For Youth lost. It's as simple as that."[28]

Not quite.

As Jack Newfield wrote at the time the disputes were raging, "It seems impossible to make a completely truthful statement about Mobilization For Youth without using the word 'but.' "[29] MFY did not (or has not) produced much sociological data, *but* was there ever such an experiment? Some persons got chewed up in it, *but* many others got their first training in an important new activity. MFY did lose in its battle with City Hall, *but* it set a pattern for the community action programs that were to spring up across the land at the very moment its own came under fire. MFY was both conscious and proud of the influence it was having. In the winter of 1964 its *News Bulletin* reported that in a two-month period in 1964, "Twenty-seven groups or individuals spent 122 hours (or an average of 4½ hours each)—the equivalent of nearly a full working month." The visitors were for the most part professionals in the field or government officials. "Time-consuming? Yes. Highly important? Again, yes, for a major objective is the flowering of Mobilization's seeds 'in other places at other times.'"[30]

The first OEO Community Action Guide, in its suggested procedures and program measures, clearly shows the influence of MFY. Preschool education, legal aid for the poor (not just to defend them, but to serve them as plaintiffs), a theory of community organization, an emphasis on research and evaluation, and most especially the insistence on the involvement of the poor, all these were the legacy of Mobilization For Youth. It was no small achievement.

There was a legacy, also, of bitterness. The men who had conceived MFY could not imagine that those involved in its symbolic demise could have acted from any but the most sinister and despicable motives. Mayor Wagner became an increasing target of savage criticism from the left, even as he was losing support among conservative voters for the enormous public expenditures he was devoting to the programs of Negro and Puerto Rican poverty. In the end he decided not to run for re-election, and turned the task over to Paul Screvane, the President of the City Council and head of the City's antipoverty board. Screvane was the one man the MFY supporters could not forgive. They were convinced that he was involved with the original *Daily News* accusations. Winslow Carlton, for example, believed, and so informed Federal officials, that Screvane had actually edited the original article.[31] Screvane had an entirely different version of events, which not surprisingly, implicated the police department. But his background—a Queens Italian, a Catholic, a sanitation man—and his personal style were antipathetical to the partisans of MFY.

Although Screvane was endorsed by the great majority of the Reform Democratic political clubs in the City, and although he was pitted against the old-line Brooklyn and Bronx organizations, which were the principal foes of the reformers, a reform slate was nonetheless put in the field against him, and in the event took away enough votes to give the primary victory to the regulars. The MFY issue was extensively used against Screvane by the liberal left.[32]

Screvane felt he had saved MFY. Cloward felt he had destroyed it and said so at length in a *Nation* article which appeared during the primary campaign that was to decide whether Screvane would become a national figure or a has-been. It cannot but be that city halls around the nation noticed. A former aide to Paul Screvane summarized the sequence to Thomas Blau as follows:[33]

. . . We lost the election for Paul Screvane by getting him into the poverty business. I knew enough about politics to know that no one could represent all the people, that is, that no one organization could really represent an entire community undisputedly. We were not going to allocate "turfs." So Paul told people, "we're not funding single organizations to the exclusion of everyone else," and so made more enemies than friends by denying the possibility of exclusive funding.

Blau is describing the difficulties political executives face in allocating public funds to the quasi-public organizations such as community action groups, which are instantly open to challenge on the grounds of representativeness. Mobilization was only the first. Yet the concept that within the mass there resided the essence of a popular will retained its power and was much in evidence in the succeeding administration. Blau comments:[34]

> In a nominalistic sense, reform in New York, like reform before it, has favored greater mass participation, but in terms of many unconnected individuals, each having no power of any importance. "Participation," either as taking part in insurgency or having an institutionalized share of authoritative decision making, may thus be a mechanism for reducing autonomy as easily as one for engendering it. Reform movements have frequently "liberated" the poor from machines, leaving them with less power than before.

A brief envoi to MFY, whose work continues, and whose stormy and vital history is yet to be written: In the summer of 1968, the City of New York, with the assistance of a Yale summer interne and the fullest cooperation, as it were, of the *New York Times,* launched a monster registration campaign in the poorer areas of the City. (Had a Tammany Mayor undertaken to spend public funds for such a purpose the *Times* might have seen the matter differently. But this was a reform Mayor, and in any event the poverty program had legitimated such efforts, and they were not yet being resorted to by outright reactionaries.) But for all the publicity, nothing much seemed to come of it. M. S. Handler reported on the first two days showing in a story headed: "Drive to Register the Poor Here Meets Indifference and Apathy." The young interne, Arthur Klebanoff, stated that campaign workers on the Lower East Side had encountered "fantastic" indifference among Puerto Ricans. Handler's report continues: [35]

He also felt that intense rivalry between community action groups had had a discouraging effect on the people. Instead of cooperating, he said, members of a group would sometimes discourage persons from registering with another more successful group, and this resulted in anger on all sides.

## NOTES

1. Jack Newfield, *New York Post,* August 30, 1964, quoting Charles Grosser.

2. Eleanor Maccoby et al., "Community Integration and the Social Control of Delinquency," *Journal of Social Issues,* 14 (1958), 38–51.

3. Morris Axelrod, "Urban Structure and Social Participation," *American Sociological Review,* 21 (February 1956), 13–18.

4. W. G. Mather, "Income and Social Participation," *American Sociological Review,* 6 (June 1947), 380–381.

5. Peter Rossi, *Why Families Move* (New York: The Free Press, 1955), p. 58.

6. MFY Prospectus, p. 126.

7. *Ibid.,* p. ix.

8. *Ibid.,* p. 198.

9. Leonard Chazen, "Participation of the Poor: Section 202 (a) (3) Organizations Under the Economic Opportunity Act of 1964," *Yale Law Journal,* 75 (March 1966), 608.

10. Richard A. Cloward and Francis Fox Piven, "Corporate Imperialism for the Poor," *The Nation,* October 16, 1967.

11. *Ibid.*

12. MFY, The Community Organization Housing Program, Report to the Ad-Hoc Committee on Community Organization, January 7, 1964, mimeographed.

13. Herbert Krosney, *Beyond Welfare, Poverty in the Supercity* (New York: Holt, Rinehart, and Winston, 1966), p. 25.

14. Quoted in *Ibid.,* p. 23.

15. See *Herald Tribune* clip in MFY folder.

16. Jack Newfield, *New York Post,* August 30, 1964.

17. Charles E. Silberman, "Pieties and Realities: Some Con-

structive Approaches to Negro-Jewish Relations." Address to the 62nd Annual Meeting of The American Jewish Committee, May 24, 1968.

18. Hubert H. Humphrey, "Race in a Changing World," American Jewish Committee, 1966, p. 11.

19. *New York Times*, May 1, 1967.

20. Max Lerner, *The Washington Evening Star*, April 19, 1967.

21. *New York Herald Tribune*, August 19, 1964.

22. In 1964 Alinsky's techniques were expounded and praised in Charles E. Silberman's widely read *Crisis in Black and White*. His final chapter, devoted to The Woodlawn Organization is entitled "The Revolt Against 'Welfare Colonialism.' "

23. Lloyd E. Ohlin, "Issues in the Development of Indigenous Social Movements Among Residents of Deprived Urban Areas," mimeographed, 1960, p. 8.

24. Paul Goodman, "Reflections on Racism, Spite, Guilt, and Violence," *New York Review of Books*, May 23, 1968, p. 21.

25. *Op. cit.*, p. 627.

26. *New York Times*, September 23, 1964.

27. *New York Times*, November 6, 1964.

28. Krosney, *Beyond Welfare, op. cit.* p. 33.

29. *New York Post*, August 30, 1964.

30. *MFY News Bulletin*, Winter, 1964.

31. Author's private papers.

32. And alas, against me as well. In the hectic political lottery of the time, I found myself in the company of Orin Lehman, running with Screvane as a team for Mayor, Comptroller, and President of the City Council. In an interview with Jack Newfield, then writing for the *Village Voice*, I talked about the MFY issue, about which I happened to know something, but in which I had not in any way been directly involved. Newfield wrote a straight account, which the *Voice* put on its front page with a large heading stating that I claimed to have "Extracted Reds from MFY." I had said nothing of the sort, and Newfield had written nothing of the sort. But then the *Village Voice* shares many qualities with the *Daily News*.

33. Thomas Blau, *On the End of Community Action: How Much Does It Matter?* Mimeographed, 1968, p. 16.

34. *Ibid.*, p. 9.

35. *New York Times*, August 15, 1968.

# CHAPTER SEVEN

# COMMUNITY
# ACTION
# LOSES

<

The 1964 election passed, the war on poverty began. By the end of January 1966, more than nine hundred grants had been made for the establishment or planning of Community Action Programs in some one thousand counties. All of the fifty largest cities in the country had CAP's. Although the richest counties had been ahead of the poorest in getting started, the latter gradually caught up. If the object had been to "cover" as many of the poor as possible with a local "umbrella" agency, the planners and administrators at OEO had done a remarkable job. Shriver's strong point was getting into position fast: no small matter in combat.

But the CAP program was not, from the point of view of its sponsors, a success. From the outset, it was in trouble. If MFY had sent out road companies (as in a sense it did), the drama could hardly have been more faithfully re-enacted in city after city across the land. There was even an extended run in rural Mississippi. This at least is an impression easily acquired.

The history of these early programs has not been written. It must be. Almost certainly a careful, detailed enquiry will turn up a great number and wide variety of innovations, changes, improvements that took place as a result of the community efforts stimulated by the Economic Opportunity Act. Some of the programs involved—Head Start, Neighborhood Legal Services—have become so familiar and popular as no longer particularly to be associated with community action, or even the war on poverty! In the manner that American advertising can transform a household appliance from a luxury to a necessity in a matter of years, almost in a matter of months OEO made preschool education a standard feature of an up-to-date community, such that any without it could properly consider themselves badly governed, deprived, or whatever.[1] Very possibly, the most important long run impact of the community action programs of the 1960's will prove to have been the formation of an urban Negro leadership echelon at just the time when the Negro masses and other minorities were verging towards extensive commitments to urban politics. Tammany at its best (or worst) would have envied the political apprenticeship provided the neighborhood coordinators of the antipoverty program. Wofford reports that in the period 1964–66 between 25 per cent and 35 per cent of the field representatives recruited for the community action program were Negro, Puerto Rican, or Mexican American. It was, he continues, "probably the ablest and largest group of minority group *professionals* ever assembled in one government program." Kenneth E. Marshall, one of the planners with Kenneth B. Clark and Cyril Tyson of HARYOU, and subsequently head of the Paterson, New Jersey, community action program agrees: "The major immediate beneficiaries of these programs," he stated in 1967, "have been non-poor persons who have been afforded the opportunity of executive, technical and professional positions in the program."[2] Saul Alinsky was more blunt, referring early in 1965 to the "vast network of sergeants drawing general's pay" in the poverty program, and noting also the speed with which apparently quite lucrative consulting firms spring up to help the indigenous disadvantaged prepare requests for grants from OEO. Even the *Wall Street Journal* took note of this new business opportunity.

The future is never to be predicted, but it would be surprising if a Namier-like history of American politics in the coming generation did not record in some detail the influence of the community action programs of the war on poverty on the personal and ideological formation of a significant number of urban political leaders. But as for the utterly disparate, but simultaneously entertained goals of program coordination and political activism, neither occurred, and in the process of not occurring, all hell broke loose all over the place.

With no detailed history available, it is hardly possible to develop a typology of the CAP's which varied considerably: some were citywide and run by City Hall; some neighborhood based and run from, if not by the neighborhood; still others took in large areas yet were relatively independent. In the first year of operation three-quarters of the community action agencies that began operations were newly established non-profit bodies, although actual control within these organizations varied. Although all manner of groups were represented, it would appear that by and large, in large cities, community action came to be primarily associated with the cause of Negro betterment.

At the risk of oversimplification, it might be said that the CAP's most closely controlled by City Hall were disappointing, and that the ones most antagonistic were destroyed. There was a large area in between, but it tended to receive little attention. For the most militant agencies, something like a four-stage sequence seems to have been followed. First, a period of organizing, with much publicity and great expectations everywhere. Second, the beginning of operations, with the onset of conflict between the agency and local government institutions, with even greater publicity. Third, a period of counterattack from local government, not infrequently accompanied by conflict and difficulties, including accounting troubles, within the agency itself. Fourth, victory for the established institutions, or at best, stalemate, accompanied by bitterness and charges of betrayal. Whatever else had occurred, the quest for community had failed.

The nub of the difficulty was that the program was nominally designed to bring about institutional cooperation, but in fact, in the words of John G. Wofford, staff assistant to the Deputy Director of the Community Action Program, the "key—and often unstated—objective of the Community Action Program [was] institutional change."[3] Chazen puts it even more bluntly: "section 202(a)(3) . . . has been commonly interpreted as a mandate for federal assistance in the effort to create political organizations for the poor."[4] Michael Harrington, whose influence among poverty workers was very considerable at this time, or so would be the impression, argued in one forum after another that the Economic Opportunity Act would—should—mean for the organization of the poor in the 1960's what the Wagner Act had meant for the organization of the industrial workers in the 1930's. That is to say, the Federal government would not do the job, but had made it much easier for others to do, not least by lending its moral authority to the enterprise. These various objectives were incompatible and proved such.

The drama was excruciatingly played out in Syracuse, New York. With the enactment of the antipoverty program, an organization originally established by the President's Committee on Juvenile Delinquency was promptly transformed into the Syracuse Crusade For Opportunity and promptly undertook to serve as an umbrella agency in the best Ylvisaker/Hackett formulation. In a city of 222,000 inhabitants, with only 16,000 Negroes, the Crusade began with a white majority on its board. Simultaneously, however, OEO gave a grant to Syracuse University to establish a Community Action Training Center to experiment with new approaches for enabling the poor to participate in the management of programs such as that of the Crusade For Opportunity. In no time, tensions were rising. As one Federal official put it to a Wall Street Journal reporter: "The community leaders felt the University was training agents provocateurs—and of course, it was." Systematic agitation began among the Negro poor, demanding that Negroes take over Crusade For Opportunity. Early in 1966 the white, Jewish executive director resigned the $19,000 job and was replaced by a militant Negro, James Tillman, Jr., who had been associate director of the University's Community Action Training Center. A year later, Negroes acquired a majority on the Board itself, and a Negro board chairman was chosen. Crusade For Opportunity "went black." It also became more and more abrasive. "How else do you gain power for the poor?" asked the new executive director. Remedial reading manuals informed their struggling "functional illiterates": "No ends are accomplished without the use of force. . . . Squeamishness about force is the mark not of idealistic, but moonstruck morals." The local NAACP charged that such materials were "geared to rioting," and called for the resignation of the new director. Militants joined the chapter and packed a meeting to denounce *its* head as a "house nigger." The turbulence steadily mounted.

This might have been well enough had there been any results to show of the kind that would justify the abrasiveness or enable the new organization to defend itself when attacked. But this would seem not to be the case. Repeated efforts to start job training programs apparently came to little. The official in charge of the program confessed in mid-1967 that it had been "a dismal failure." Nor were there any political payoffs for advocates of social change. The Republican Mayor was easily re-elected in 1965, not only in spite of but, in the view of local observers, largely *because* of the intense opposition, even harassment, directed against him by the various poverty groups. Nor does there appear to have been any very great deal of actual participation by the poor in the operation of the poverty agency. Those who got hold of it seem to have been secretive and jealous of power. And then finances became a scandal. To the doubtless immense satisfaction of the conservative Irish, Italian, and German working-class groups of the city, the Negroes turned out to have been running Crusade For Opportunity with all the concern for niceties of a Reconstruction legislature. Of some $8 million expended by mid-1967, about $7 million had gone for salaries. Just what the poor got out of it was hard to see. In July, 1967, for the first time anywhere, OEO placed the Syracuse community action program in trusteeship. Two white and one Negro trustees were appointed.

Later that year, in the crucial November debates in the House of Representatives over the future of OEO, Rep. James M. Hanley, a Syracuse Democrat elected in the Johnson sweep in 1964 spoke on the floor of the importance of greater local government involvement in poverty programs. A sensible and sensitive representative of the long (and decidedly mixed) tradition of Irish politics in the city, all he asked of the poverty program was what the PCJD and the Ford Foundation had promised. Speaking of Crusade for Opportunity, he said:[5]

The Crusade did not assume the responsibility to effectively and efficiently manage and administer the program grants awarded by the OEO. But most of all, the old community action agency *failed to mobilize all of the resources of the community* to wage an effective war on poverty. Many battles were fought, but few were against poverty. [My italics.]

This was a recurrent theme of not unsympathetic observers of big city community action programs elsewhere in the nation. In June 1965, in an article entitled "More Shouting than Shooting," Paul Weeks of the *Los Angeles Times* (June 13, 1965) described the situation in that city weeks before the great riot:

Nowhere . . . has the turn in the war from fighting the enemy to fighting over who is going to run the war been more evident than in the Los Angeles area. . . . The frontal assault on deprivation has been reduced to sporadic fire while a showdown rages behind the lines over who are going to be the generals and who will be the privates.

Seemingly it comes to this. Over and again, the attempt by official and quasi-official agencies (such as the Ford Foundation) to organize poor communities led first to the radicalization of the middle-class persons who began the effort; next to a certain amount of stirring among the poor, but accompanied by heightened racial antagonism *on the part of the poor* if they happened to be black; next to retaliation from the larger white community; whereupon it would emerge that the community action agency, which had talked so much, been so much in the headlines, promised so much in the way of change in the fundamentals of things, was powerless. A creature of a Washington bureaucracy, subject to discontinuation without notice. Finally, much bitterness all around. Just possibly, the philanthropists and socially concerned intellectuals never took seriously enough their talk about the "power structure." Certainly, they seemed repeatedly to assume that those who had power would let it be taken away a lot easier than could possibly be the case if what was involved was *power*. Dismissed from his post, sitting at home surrounded by African artifacts, James Till- man, Jr., may have spoken more truly than he knew in describing what had happened to him. Speaking of himself in the third person, he put it thus:[6]

Tillman happens to be a social engineer, and understands fear. Only real patricians can give up power easily, while nouveau riche resent any inroads on their authority. There obviously aren't any patricians in Syracuse.

Technically he was wrong. Decision-making in Syra- cuse is as diffuse a process as in most medium Amer- ican cities, yet to a pronounced degree events there are influenced by a fairly small number of men in banks and law firms whose names are not generally known, who do not run for Congress, who do not run for mayor. It may be that Tillman had not met them; he would not in that event describe them as especially nouveau, but neither would he have concluded they were patricians. They were and remain the tough power brokers of an American city, and they can out- wait a black "agent provocateur" anytime *if* that individual is dependent on the House of Representatives and the General Accounting Office to stay in business.

In a number of instances the demise of the community action organization has been prevented by a transfer of leadership from political or racial militants to social welfare professionals. This happened at MFY, and also at HARYOU. But the results were not necessarily different as to social change, nor were the difficulties of simply running a large organization avoided. Early in 1968, Kenneth E. Marshall, speaking of HARYOU, charged before the Community Council of Greater New York that "none of it worked." Charles H. King, a 47-year-old social worker who had been appointed director of the program early in 1967, agreed that the indices of "social pathology" which had been laid out in 1964 as a measure of the social situation were still worsening in Central Harlem. He insisted, however, and correctly, that HARYOU had never got the funding it anticipated. Even so, the question was to be asked what had it done with what it had got. In July 1968 the president of the HARYOU board, Marshall England announced that he would ask for a Federal investigation of the agency. The clear implication of his statement was that funds were being misused. At a 12-hour board meeting preceding his statement, a pistol and tear gas were discharged. Returning to his own office, England received a telephone call warning him to "stay out of the HARYOU office or you'll be killed."[7] The conclusion seems unavoidable: the programs were at once too big, and not big enough, and where Negro communities were involved, constituted a devastating form of what had by then come to be known as "white colonialist imperialism."

It may be that the poor are never "ready" to assume power in an advanced society: the exercise of power in an effective manner is an ability acquired through apprenticeship and seasoning. Thrust on an individual or a group, the results are often painful to observe, and when what in fact is conveyed is not power, but a kind of playacting at power, the results can be absurd. The devise of holding elections among the poor to choose representatives for the CAP governing boards made the program look absurd. The turnouts in effect declared that the poor weren't interested: in Philadelphia 2.7 per cent; Los Angeles 0.7 per cent; Boston 2.4 per cent; Cleveland 4.2 per cent; Kansas City, Mo. 5.0 per cent.[8] Smaller communities sometimes got larger turnouts, but never anything nearly approaching that of a listless off-year election. (If theory held the poor to be apathetic, why proceed as if this were not so? In the Democratic primary election of 1968, with the election of the first Negro Congressman from Brooklyn at issue, a mere 11,825 votes were cast in the 12th Congressional district, comprising the Bedford Stuyvesant area, compared to 43,940 in the adjacent 13th district.) Once elected or chosen, the representatives do not seem to have been especially effective. Rubin, a wholly sympathetic observer, writes: "The Boards have been rent by endless quarrels, born of a basic lack of understanding of the differentiation between policy-making and administrative functions."[9] As Negroes grew more militant, the impression would be that more and more white executives were forced out of the programs, but this only precipitated intensive struggles for place among blacks. Community action salaries were often extraordinarily high in terms of what was otherwise available to the Negro middle class, and the struggle was often bitter, with all the accoutrement of charge, countercharge, and scandal. In Harlem, for example, it was the local Negro newspaper that led the campaign against the executive salary structure in HARYOU-ACT. Irony: patronage, which was the source of stability in the original ethnic neighborhood political organization, became a source of instability in the contrived organizations created to fill the gap left by the destruction of the real thing.

A final verdict *must* be withheld. But interim ones are available, and by and large they have been negative. Bayard Rustin, for example, speaks of the "bedlam of community action programs" and clearly suggests they have made organized "ghetto" political activity more difficult, not less. S. M. Miller and Pamela Roby, of the Ford Foundation, conclude that OEO, far from creating a constituency and bringing about institutional change, has in fact brought about little change, produced few supporters, and has brought on "enormous dissatisfaction." All the result of "maximum feasible participation" for which "civil rights and other groups were not effectively organized" despite the best efforts of OEO.[10]

Within CAP's the struggle for control frequently acquired bitter ideological and generation aspects. Thus in 1966 the executive director and three high staff members of the $8 million Youth in Action program in New York's Bedford-Stuyvesant area resigned in fury, charging the board of directors with being "middle class oriented," shaking the organization very considerably.[11] That Cloward and Ohlin would have hoped for nothing better than a middle-class oriented local board giving youth opportunities was a detail long since obscured. In a city such as New York where the poor are not so exclusively Negro, the potential for ethnic conflict for control over the CAP's, especially within the framework of the election of poor representatives, provided plentiful opportunities for ethnic hostility. Negro-Puerto Rican battles raged within New York City's antipoverty program. Under the administration of John V. Lindsay, Mitchell Sviridoff who had headed the community action program in New Haven, was brought in to run New York's program. Ethnic conflict was immediate. In 1967, Herman Badillo, the Puerto Rican-born Borough President of the Bronx declared of the local election scheme:[12]

> In effect, they are taking the poverty program and making it like a political campaign with winner take all. When you say that whoever gets 51 per cent is going to control the program, you put a premium on groups vying for control, and that's not going to lead to people working together.

At his side, Percy Sutton, the Negro Borough President of Manhattan, nodded assent. Two unusually gifted and successful elected officials, working in the tradition of New York ethnic politics, their shared view, contrasting as they do with those of the professional reformer is to be noted.

Before long, ideological, generational, and ethnic problems were compounded by the familiar ones of bureaucracy. An administrative study of OEO is much needed, especially with respect to the degree to which under the banner of community control, the essential decisions about local affairs came increasingly to be made in Washington via the direct CAP-OEO line of communication and funding. But rigidities of the more familiar kind early made their appearance. In 1967, Wofford asked whether the one thousand community action agencies around the country were becoming a new bureaucracy that would "stifle change" and have to be superceded. The following year George Nicolau, stepping down after running for 18 months the largest community action agency in the nation, declared himself "a victim of that process which in the space of three short years created and has almost been overwhelmed by its own complexties and its own bureaucracy."[13]

A final irony, and in its many ramifications a fateful one, is that the Federal antipoverty warriors, for all their desperately good intentions, got precious little thanks. Each local conflict solved seemed to bear the seeds of the next one. Wofford describes the process: a mayor undertakes to step up a community action program under his own control; a pressure group, the "***Committee for a More Effective Community Action Program" is formed to demand that the poor be given greater participation; the Mayor forms a new community action agency and makes the head of the pressure group the executive director; the new director is denounced for having sold out to the white power structure; the "***Committee for an Even More Effective Community Action Program" is formed.[14]

With militancy the mark of merit and increasingly measured in terms of the ability to be sufficiently outrageous to obtain press and television coverage—or so one is forced to conclude from the behavior of those involved—more and more the antipoverty program came to be associated with the kind of bad manners and arrogance that are more the mark of the rich than the poor, or perhaps more accurately, the too-common attributes of the radical right and left. Shriver's experience with the Citizens Crusade Against Poverty is not unrepresentative. Early on, the need for a constituency for OEO became evident. Further, Reuther by 1965 was more and more attracted by the possibility of organizing "community unions," freeing the labor movement from its confines of work place and craft, "providing the poor with their own self-sufficient economic organization in their community." With a $1 million pledge from the UAW, 125 organizations were brought together in November 1965, and the Citizens Crusade Against Poverty was founded, ostensibly to give OEO support, possibly to create an atmosphere for an organizing campaign. (Bayard Rustin's vision of a coalition of labor, liberal, and civil rights forces was much in mind.) Boone left OEO to become executive director. A prestigious board was assembled, complete with bona fide representatives of the poor. In 1966 a great meeting was held in Washington. Shriver appeared, but far from receiving support, he was hooted, booed, jostled, and verbally attacked. The predominantly Negro audience remained passive while a militant minority raged at the director of OEO. "He hasn't done anything for us," cried one delegate, "Where do the poor have an opportunity?" "It's just a big publicity deal," shouted another. "We aren't being heard because we don't have the money." "The poverty program is a laugh," declared a mother of six from Watts. "When all the money is spent, the rich will get richer and I will still be receiving a welfare check."[15]

Seven months later, on December 22nd, a busload of what the *New York Times* called "the vocal poor and their representatives" made their way to Timberlawn, Shriver's home in suburban Washington, where much of the antipoverty program had been planned, and where he and his family were gathered for the Christmas holidays. Carols were sung:

> Hark the Herald Angels sing
> Glory to the newborn king.
> Sing of peace forever more,
> While the poor finance the war.
> Shriver go to L.B.J.
> Tell him what the poor folk say.
> Charity begins at home.
> We want gigs to call our own.
> Young adults are on the roam
> Soon we'll have a war at home.
>
> O come all ye poor folk,
> Soulful and together
> Come ye, O come ye to Shriver's house.

141

Come and behold him, politicians' puppet.
O come and let us move him,
O come and sock it to him,
And send him on his way to L.B.J.

Keep the money in the kitty,
   Fa la la la la la la la la
Let's get down to nitty gritty
   Fa la la la la la la la la
Put us poor folks in the cold,
   Fa la la la la la la la la
Shriver you ain't got no soul,
   Fa la la la la la la la la

The painful quality about these demonstrations, and their counterparts in city after city across the land, is that at base they depended on the power of the weak: the power to disrupt, to embarrass, to provoke, to goad to punitive rage, but banking (usually) on the inhibitions, personal or collective, of those goaded. A gentleman does not strike a lady. But neither does the heart grow fonder in consequence of the restraint imposed by the unequal contest that would ensue. What all this told the White House was that the antipoverty program was becoming a political liability. It patently had few friends among mayors, few among congressmen, and now with the seemingly inexorable logic of conflict stimulation, few among the poor. A few months after the episode at Timberlawn, President Johnson confided to a member of the Senate Committee on Labor and Public Welfare that it was hardly his favorite program. He need not have been so cautious: the fact was painfully evident throughout Washington.

About all that can be said with confidence concerning the President's attitude toward the antipoverty program is that it may be depended upon to have been complex. A further judgment, for which some information exists, is that there was to his mind a fairly clear distinction between the categorical programs of OEO

142

—employment for youth, loans for small farmers, education for pre-school children—concepts familiar from the days of the National Youth Administration of the New Deal, when he began his political career as a counterpart of the OEO antipoverty warriors of the 1960's, and the community action programs. (A fact to be noted: Texas in the 1960's had the largest number of poor persons defined by Social Security Administration standards, of any state in the union: 2,970,350 in 1960.) His attitude toward community action appears to have been one of instant suspicion and dislike. He appears to have judged that it would encounter exactly the political troubles it did run into, that is to say that it would cause troubles for his friends rather than his enemies. He had no sympathy whatever for financing a conflict of the Democratic poor against the Democratic mayors of the nation, and that, repeatedly, is what community action brought about in simple consequence of both the Negro masses and most of the urban mayors being Democratic. In a manner of many persons whose lives have been involved with government, he appears to have been uneasy with the notion of turning government funds and programs over to nongovernmental corporations. He confided to at least one Senator that something of the sort was tried on two occasions in Texas during the New Deal and was quickly put a stop to by Roosevelt. In any event, it was the judgment of OEO officials closest to the community action program that in the President's mind the question was settled before the program even began: he wanted no disruption. In meetings at his Texas ranch immediately following the 1964 election he made his position clear.

At first it would seem the surprising thing is that community action marched forth to battle nonetheless. But this would miss the essential point: neither Shriver nor anyone else at the top of the OEO command—including Conway—seems to have anticipated the turmoil. For Shriver, the Peace Corps analogy was obviously influential. Everyone loved the Peace Corps. For Conway, the example of the industrial unions was uppermost. The most ferocious rhetoric merely preceded a lucrative and mutually agreeable settlement. As for rank and file revolt, the worst that ever happened was a brief wildcat strike over washroom rights. For the rest, the Ylvisaker-Hackett concept of coordination was uppermost, and unchallenged. This point is crucial: *conflict* may be thought of as the dynamic of community organization, as what leaders induce or followers demand once the program is mounted, but *coordination* remained the expectation of the Washington administrators. Long after he had left the scene, Hackett insisted that coordination was the function of community action. Long after it had been seen that coordination is what rarely occurred, the job title of the Federal man in the neighborhood was—community coordinator. Thus in a sense, no one knew how to respond to the President's concerns.

Save the Bureau of the Budget. There, disillusion with the "OEO radicals," as they came to be known in some circles at least of the Executive Office Building, was instantaneous. The Bureau had been promised coordination, and all it has seemingly got was chaos; *ergo,* cut back funds. In the second fiscal year of the antipoverty program, beginning July 1, 1965, community action received 45 per cent of the total appropriation, altogether $685 million. But by the spring of that year protests from city governments about the tactics of the new community action agencies were already pouring in. The issue was policymaking. Mayor Richard J. Daley of Chicago was known to be mightily upset. In the correct tradition of urban, Democratic, ethnic politics, the Chicago antipoverty program was roaring ahead, and predictably became a champion grabber and distributor of antipoverty funds. The party was looking after the people. What was not distributed, however, was the power to make such allocations. Do that and one day you wake up and there is no machine. Mayor Daley wanted the poor to be employed *by* the program. *He* wanted to make the decisions about it. From the point of view of the tradition of working class politics, his position was impeccable. From the point of view of the middle class liberals who devised and now ran the antipoverty program, it was sinister, evil, hateful. Inevitably, the President sided with the Mayor. In the spring, a group of mayors, led by Daley, met with Vice President Humphrey and voiced their concern. The Bureau of the Budget needed hardly to be persuaded. And thus almost at the outset the Executive Office of the President began to exert a steady pressure on OEO to keep the community action programs as quiet as possible, which in effect meant to keep the role of the poor in policymaking to a minimum.

This effort first became public the following fall. On November 5, 1965, a front-page story appeared in *The New York Times*, stating:

> The Budget Bureau, fiscal arm of the White House, has told the Office of Economic Opportunity that it would prefer less emphasis on policy-making by the poor in planning community projects.
>
> "Maximum feasible participation" by the poor in the antipoverty program is called for by the law. In the bureau's view, this means primarily using the poor to carry out the program, not to design it.

The immediate issue was that the Bureau was holding back $35 million of the Title II appropriation, but the generalized antagonism was clear. The story, written by Joseph A. Loftus, an experienced journalist, was clearly leaked from OEO. Towards the end, it noted that there were a number of cities where local government completely dominated the community action program, but that even there OEO was promulgating procedures whereby neighborhood groups could obtain money from OEO without having to go through city hall. Loftus noted: [16]

This memorandum had been circulating inside the agency for more than a month. Then it was redrafted and distributed to the city antipoverty agencies. There was no accompanying announcement here.

The "OEO radicals," in a word, were fighting back—taking their story to the public; concealing their moves from their superiors—the familiar Washington sequence. The not less familiar outcome is that the Bureau of the Budget wins. It can afford to wait. The next day, from the Texas White House, Bill D. Moyers, Press Secretary to the President, confirmed that the Bureau had indeed "raised with the Office of Economic Opportunity the question of the extent to which the poor should be involved in policy planning. But no advice that less participation would be advisable was given."[17]

Neither the White House, nor the Executive Office of the President had expected anything like the situation then developing. Nor had the Shriver task force that conceived OEO. The task force had wanted to ensure that Southern Negroes got their share of the benefits, and it was responsive to the notion that the poor, if employed in the program, might be more effective in dealing with their counterparts than the traditional bourgeois social worker. But as Yarmolinsky later stated, there was no intention of getting the poor "to think of themselves as a political force." It did not, he continued, "occur to us, and it didn't occur to any of the highly professional politicians we consulted."[18] It certainly did not occur to the Congress.

In part, this can be ascribed to a cultural phenomenon: the difference between the New York mind and the Washington mind. Community action, in both its conservative and radical formulations, was a product of New York. The war on poverty was a product of Washington. The one deeply concerned with society, the other preoccupied with government; the one emotionally no less than ideologically committed to social change, the other profoundly attached to the artifacts of stability and continuity; the one fascinated by racial, ethnic, and religious diversity; the other fiercely loyal to the Republic and still trying to fashion a nation out of a continent. It is a contrast between ideas and information, between brilliance and endurance, between innovation and preservation. A contrast between the New York School of Social Work housed in Andrew Carnegie's mansion on Fifth Avenue, and the Bureau of the Budget ensconced in the magnificent old State, War, and Navy building "across the street," as they say, from the White House. The difference is to be seen in the bookstores, the restaurants, the ferocity, even vulgarity, of the teeming cultural life of the great metropolis, as against the somehow embarrassing efforts to keep alive in Washington one-each, a modern art gallery, a symphony orchestra, a repertory theater. Finally there is the profound difference in the sense of security of the two cities, in the feeling of how much threat and demonstration can be tolerated. The civil rights march on Washington of August 1963 began in New York, in the sense that it was organized there. No one gave it a thought. But on the day it arrived in Washington the bars were closed and something between a third and a half of the civil service stayed home from work.

This contrast between the cultural and the political capitals has rarely been more acute than during the three years that followed the enactment of the Economic Opportunity Act. The twin issues of the Negro revolution and the war in Vietnam were at the base of it, but also the personality of Lyndon Johnson, the first President to have spent his entire adult life in Washington, the company town of the American Republic. Johnson, in effect, drifted into a Washington-New York confrontation. And he lost. His administration was toppled by the literary reviews, the salons, the intellectual élite ("West Side Jacobins," he was repeatedly reassured: nothing to fear), the cultural arbiters of New York who, during this period determined that his course in foreign policy was a disaster. Simultaneously, for reasons that may or may not be connected, the Negro slums of the nation erupted in violence. Desperately committed to Vietnam, Johnson had no funds with which to respond to what was manifestly a problem of poverty. He responded instead with commissions of enquiry of various kinds. Repeatedly his commissions would tell him he had to spend more, just as repeatedly his Secretary of the Treasury told him there was no money. The war went badly; violence spread to the middle classes, the country was approaching instability; the President resigned.

But not before coming to loathe and fear the forces that had been let loose by the antipoverty program, an anxiety to which a certain measure of country boy credulity in the White House staff—combined often as not with intelligence and an intense capacity for public service—often contributed.

The Southern Protestant quality of the White House

under Johnson was nowhere more painfully evident than in its dealings with the political left. It was at once far too willing to assume that the movement had withered away and, intermittently, altogether too much alarmed at discovering this not to be the case. Thus in the fall of 1967, with the antipoverty program fighting for its life, some circles at least in the White House were taking seriously a report in *Barron's National Business and Financial Weekly* on the Third Conference of Socialist Scholars that had recently met in New York City. In terms of purest hysteria, the author of the article, described as an "authority on the so-called Left, Old and New alike," divulged the theretofore closely held confidence that Michael Harrington was a socialist. Not only a socialist but, the article continued, in the course of an afternoon panel discussion at the Statler Hilton Hotel, he shifted from the Menshevik to Bolshevik variety. This conversion was the work of one Stanley Aronowitz, chairman of Manhattan's West Side Committee for Independent Political Action. Nor was Harrington's the only secret to surface on the occasion. The article continues: [19]

> Violently, Aronowitz attacked the entire Poverty Program except for a single aspect which he described as "a valuable tool" for the radical movement. "At least," he said, "it has given employment to the organizers."
> The audience burst into laughter, applause and cheers. "That's right, man" called out someone from the floor. "It gave our organizers some bread." In leftist slang, bread means money.

The article is not altogether absurd. Any White House aide might at this point have been upset at the violence of the rhetoric emerging from some of the community action organizers. But three years earlier, when the program was just beginning, Charles M. Silberman in a speech in Washington had declared that the concept of community action as a government-sponsored program entailed "the bankruptcy of the left." It would not work, he said; it could not. It would leave everyone bitter and distrustful. But the White House simply could not understand what he was talking about. Bankruptcy of what left?

If the administration was upset, Congress was aghast. Again, a cultural element is involved. The style of Congress is essentially Southern; its essence is to conceal power, not to flaunt it. And to flaunt powerlessness is a notion beyond the ken of most of the influential legislators. Thus the style of the community action militants was utterly antipathetical. Beyond this, it posed serious political problems. The Democratic majority in the House, especially in its ranking hierarchy, consists essentially of urban liberal Democrats and Southern rural conservatives. *Both* were uniquely threatened by a seemingly government-sponsored effort to politicize the black masses of the Northern cities and the Southern countryside. Blackstone Rangers in Chicago, Child Development in Mississippi, Black Arts Theater in Harlem, all spelled trouble, and for liberal and conservative alike. As Negro rioting grew endemic, the association between community action and violence also grew in the minds of the legislators, or so it would appear. (Of course, a strong case can be and was made by OEO that the community action agencies helped control violence, but in a time of troubles these relationships grow confused.) In no time at all, the antipoverty program was in trouble in the Congress, and the focus of this trouble was community action and the provision for "maximum feasible participation" of the poor.

The response of the Congress, though a matter of intense concern to those involved with the antipoverty program and to those for whom it was designed, was fairly routine. Congress reacted much as it could have been expected. It moved to limit and to restrict the funds available to the program and simultaneously to restrain the freedom of action of its administrators. A page-one story in *The New York Times* of December 12, 1966 neatly encapsulates the process. The lead paragraph reads: [20]

Without a word of debate, the House voted today to give the Office of Economic Opportunity $370 million less than it had authorized for the agency yesterday.

Further down, the dispatch reports:

Regarding funds for the antipoverty program, the Office of Economic Opportunity said that the House not only cut its funds but also cut its discretion. As a result, it said, community action programs would have to bear the brunt of the money reduction.

Describing the 1967 sequence, Sar A. Levitan put it: [21]

If political scientists are right and the House of Representatives is a true barometer of the nation's thinking, it would seem that among the majority of the people there is a growing disillusionment with efforts to fight poverty. . . . In November 1967, the House expended over 400,000 words in debate on the extension of the Economic Opportunity Act. It succeeded in emasculating some of the old programs, adding little that promises to be constructive. The major blow was an authorization for antipoverty spending of $460 million less than requested by the President.

The antipoverty program succeeded foreign aid as the leading cliffhanger in the appropriation process. (Note in the preceding extract from the *Times* that Congress was only then, in December, appropriating funds for the fiscal year that had begun July 1, nearly six months earlier. In the interval, agencies lived at the level of their previous budget.) Rather like the foreign aid program in its earlier stages, the program was repeatedly saved in the closing hours of Congress, and the size of the total appropriations was never seriously reduced. But increasingly the funds were earmarked for specific activities such as Head Start or Neighborhood Legal Services, so that in addition to the program restrictions implicit in the various titles of the act, further limits on administrative discretion were imposed. Still, OEO had acquired defenders as well, and the process achieved a measure of equilibrium. A page-one story in the *Times* in the early summer of 1968 illustrates the pattern: [22]

John W. Gardner pleaded with Congress today to lead the nation out of "a crisis that could tear us apart." He wrote to each member "on the express instruction of 38 prominent Americans who form the Urban Coalition Action Council," of which he is chairman.

The former Secretary of Health, Education and Welfare appealed specifically against budget cuts for antipoverty jobs, housing and education.

\* \* \* \* \*

The Office of Economic Opportunity budget had been cut in committee from $2.1-billion to $1.8-billion and barely escaped a further cut of $100-million on the House floor.

\* \* \* \* \*

The Senate, on the other hand, added yesterday for the second time $75-million for summer jobs and $25-million for supplementary Head Start (preschool poverty) funds to another appropriation bill. House conferees balked at those items in an earlier appropriation bill, and left the bill to perish.

The Johnson administration was repeatedly placed in a difficult position by these threatened budget cuts. In its own internal budget process it repeatedly limited the amount of money allocated to the antipoverty program because of the requirements of the Vietnam war. This was well enough known, so that its protests against further cuts were less than fully convincing.

At times the Budget Bureau appears to have withheld from OEO part even of that money appropriated to it. Toward the end of December 1966, Melvin R. Laird, chairman of the House Republican Conference and ranking minority member of the Health, Education and Welfare subcommittee of the Appropriations Committee, publicly taunted Shriver to persuade the President to ask for more money for the antipoverty program, guaranteeing his own support if such a request was made. None was.

The move to restrict the powers of the director of OEO and the mandate of the community action agencies began early in 1966. Significantly, the prime movers were liberal, urban, northern Democrats on the House Committee on Education and Labor, men of the quality of Frank Thompson, Jr. of New Jersey and James O'Hara of Michigan. Partly from concern for their own positions, which were threatened or appeared about to be by the new agencies, and partly to forestall worse action by more conservative members, a group began to meet with Powell in the early spring for the purpose of revising the statute. Loftus of *The New York Times* got wind of it and broke the story April 28, 1966:

Leading House Democrats have agreed on amendments that will alter the face and character of the Great Society's campaign against poverty.

They are the majority of the Education and Labor Committee. They have been meeting secretly and will be ready in a few days to confront the Republicans with a Democratic consensus.

The changes are aimed straight at the Community Action Program, which Sargent Shriver last month called "the prime offensive weapon in the war on poverty."

It is one of eight major programs directed by Mr. Shriver. . . . Politically it is by far the most explosive program because it is the only one that requires "maximum feasible participation" by representatives of poverty areas. . . .

*153*

The issue of policy participation by the poor has generated "ugly problems of the political establishment" in the private language of one House Democrat who is supporting the changes.

"Extremist groups have seized it as a forum for dissent," he said.

The Democrats planned to cut the size of the community action program, limit the salary levels that might be paid in it, and increase the amount local communities would have to contribute to obtain the Federal matching grant, which had originally been 90 per cent. But when the move became public, Chairman Powell received enough protests to be forced to deny it—community action agencies could protest to Congress as well as to City Hall. This capacity of community action agencies to cause trouble for urban liberal Democrats did not escape Republican notice where, under the influence of Melvin R. Laird, a flexible and alert minority opposition was developing. Nothing came of the Democratic plans for amending the Economic Opportunity Act in 1966, but a Republican proposal sponsored by Albert H. Quie of Minnesota was adopted *requiring* that the poor make up one-third of the boards of community action agencies! Fish in troubled waters.

The Economic Opportunity Act of 1966 was signed on election day, by the close of which Republicans had gained forty-five seats in the House of Representatives, almost all of them from liberal Democrats. With that event, the Johnson administration lost the near-to-automatic majority for liberal programs which had persisted for almost three years. It was understood by all that the antipoverty program, which had become a focus of conservative opposition to the Great Society, was in trouble. By the turn of the year, informed opinion within the agency itself was that the battle was all but lost.

The administration, which shared not a few of the conservative views on this subject, sought to keep control of matters by itself taking the initiative. In March, the President sent to the Congress a special message in which he spoke only of a "strategy against poverty." The nation was fighting a war in Asia: one war was enough. He asked for seven amendments to the Economic Opportunity Act, of which the first four applied directly to community action:[23]

1. To help local community action agencies define their purpose more precisely and improve their planning, auditing and personnel systems.

2. To give public officials and other interested groups in the community voice in forming policy for community action agencies.

3. To strengthen the role of the states, especially in rural areas.

4. To encourage more participation by private enterprise.

In April the administration made known more of the specifics it would seek, again amendments primarily directed to community action: Marjorie Hunter, another *New York Times* reporter who had followed the poverty issue from its outset, summarized:[24]

The proposed changes would bar antipoverty workers from partisan political activity, rule out use of Federal funds for "illegal picketing or demonstrations," screen out troublemakers from the Job Corp, and require annual audits of all antipoverty programs.

Congressional conservatives were not appeased by these moves. Their desire, and increasingly the general expectation, was that OEO should be abolished, with its more popular programs, such as Head Start, transferred to established departments. Even Boone proposed that OEO be renamed the Office for Community Action Against Poverty and stripped of all its functions save the CAP's.[25] Shriver asserted, "The war on poverty is not fought on any single, simple battlefield and it will not be won in a generation."[26]

The summer rioting made matters worse, or so it seemed. The Newark riot was a source of considerable embarrassment. Although it was generally agreed that the United Community Corporation had not sponsored the demonstration in front of the Fourth Precinct House on July 13, following which the riot began, that as the director Donald F. Wendell put it, "We had made a decision on that Thursday morning that a demonstration was not really judicious," neither was it much disputed that UCC employees had been among the demonstrators, or that leaflets calling for the gathering had been run off on UCC equipment. After the riot, the Mayor of Newark, Hugh J. Adonizzio charged the agency with stirring up dissent. In August, OEO itself tried to suspend a director of UCC who had urged Negroes to arm themselves against whites, but gave up after Shriver concluded that as an "elected official" he could not be removed.[27] The involvement of radical white students from the Students for a Democratic Society did not help. The subsequent outbreak in Detroit, with its unquestionably distinguished mayor and model antipoverty program, complicated matters all over again. What good was coming of it all? In an October appropriation bill, the House excluded OEO employees from an otherwise across-the-board Federal pay raise, and began the systematic fiscal harrassment of the OEO itself.

And yet, as the summer wore on, the opposition to OEO did not much grow, while support for it did. OEO itself promoted a fair amount of this support. In the community action agencies it possessed, in effect, local lobbies in strategic locations throughout the country. But also, the war on poverty had won supporters on its merits, especially those of the special purpose activities such as Head Start. In response to an early enquiry

by Carl D. Perkins, who had succeeded Powell as chairman of the House Committee on Education and Labor,
big and small city mayors alike were hostile to the
CAP's. But then second thoughts seemed to take hold
and a fundamental fact emerged: community action
agencies appear to have found their way into the system of local government in many, at least, of the
nation's cities. If they were abolished the mayors would
have to find something to replace them—a familiar
situation once a federal program gets established. The
primary function of the CAP's being to reach the now
hostile and threatening minority populations, it appeared increasingly foolish to tamper. Besides which,
OEO maintained a fairly steady flow of money into
local enterprises. Evidently an adaptive process had
been at work. With the full support of the White House
and the sufficient compliance of OEO, mayors—Democrats and Republicans alike—had been learning to live
with the CAP's, finding ways to make use of them, to
incorporate them into the structure of civic governance. Of a sudden they realized it might be difficult to
live without them, especially in administering the host
of neighborhood programs that OEO had invented.

The attitude of Rep. Phillip M. Landrum at this time
suggests the degree to which the antipoverty program,
and even community action had acquired a quality of
"normalcy." In an interview in October 1967 Landrum
offered his judgment that there had been instances
where community action agencies had "gone off in
directions that are just simply not good for our form
of government." He allowed that things looked suspi-
cious in Newark, that he had heard of a husband and
wife on one community action team who had been
"closely connected with the Communist Party, and are
now associated with an organization somewhat alien
to our principles," he thought it fairly ridiculous that
one CAP had purchased telescopic sights for high-

powered rifles "and gave the excuse that they were going to be used for microscopes. He felt there would have to be "sharp revisions in the law" and some "dramatic shakeups" in personnel. Nonetheless, all that this came down to was a judgment that "we must find some way to have elected officials participate in order to give the public an avenue to get at the things which are wrong."[28]

The result was that OEO and community action survived. Again it was a cliffhanger—the Economic Act of 1967 was signed December 23—but this time delay had been rather a matter of policy. Perkins, a skilled and responsible legislator, kept putting off a showdown in the House, and in the end proved right. Community action was the issue. The key move was an amendment submitted by Rep. Edith Green which provided that local governments would have the option of bringing their community action agency under official control, always providing that a third of the representatives on its board be poor, and with bypass powers available to the director. Charles E. Goodell, an active and informed Republican member of the Committee on Education and Labor, made the tactical error of taunting the Democrats for their "bosses and boll weevil amendment," referring to the scarcely concealed intent of the move to enable the established political powers of the Southern countryside and the Northern cities to take control of community action. United in their sense of having been insulted, the Democratic majority bestirred itself and in a rush of activity adopted the amendment, authorized a two-year extension of the Economic Opportunity Act, thus relieving it of the annual ordeal of the Aid Program, and even increased its appropriation to $1.773 billion.

The war on poverty was no longer the *dernier cri* among the bright young people of Washington, the future of OEO remained in doubt, but the antipoverty program and the antipoverty posture of the American national government had begun to acquire aspects of permanency. Six months later, Joseph A. Califano, Jr., Special Assistant to President Johnson, reported that of 898 community action agencies whose courses had been determined since the Green amendment was enacted, only 48 had been taken over by City Hall. It began to appear that community action had survived: a new institution of sorts had been added to the system of American local government.

The extent of the change that took place in, roughly, the decade between the conception of Mobilization for Youth and the enactment of the Economic Opportunity Act of 1967 can be gathered from the position taken in *Republican Papers,* a volume edited by the redoubtable Melvin R. Laird, which appeared in the summer of 1968. In it, Charles E. Goodell and Albert H. Quie, who had been waiting for Shriver when he appeared with the first draft legislation on March 16, 1964, describe "The Republican Opportunity Crusade As An Alternative to the Anti-Poverty Program"; they begin with a statement of their "basic approach": [29]

The key to success of any national poverty program lies in finding the proper role of the federal government in the sophisticated society of the late twentieth century. Government programs must incorporate certain basic tenets:

1. The poor themselves must be energized through participation in planning, policy formulation and program implementation;

2. The total community with all its constituent resources must be mobilized;

3. The effort of all levels of government must be supplementary to this independent action.

The Economic Opportunity Act proposed in 1964 by President Johnson touched around the edges of these concepts but failed to incorporate them clearly and provide for their effective implementation.

What Goodell and Quie in effect declare is that the position of the "OEO radicals" on "maximum feasible participation" was the correct one, and that the work of the Shriver task force was flawed to the extent that it did not comprehend and embrace the full implications of that term! (The much-abused Yarmolinsky is cited to the effect that the Shriver task force saw the poor as working in the program, not as running it.) What is more, the Republican representatives continue, "By 1966 a Democratic coalition of Southern governors and big city machines had formed [which] . . . sought increasing control by local community action boards." Republicans fought back on behalf of the poor, but to no avail beyond the Quie amendment. The Democratic majority had its ruthless way. "Fueled by local political reaction, their drive culminated in regressive curtailment of community action in the 1967 law." Nonetheless these young, gifted, Republican politicians, in their program and their vocabulary—"opportunity," "mobilization," "coordination,"—had become true converts.

There is more to this than merely the exploitation of division and hypocrisy among Democrats. As in the writings of Nisbet and Goodman, so also in the politics of conservative Republicans and radical reformers: a certain coming together in opposition to, in distaste for, bigness, impersonality, bureaucratized benevolence, prescribed surveillance.

Not surprisingly, it was to precisely this problem that Gunnar Myrdal, in ways the most objective and hopeful of contemporary observers of American institutions, pointed in the Storrs Lectures at the Yale Law School in 1958, roughly midpoint between *The Quest for Community* and the Quie amendment. In a section entitled "The Quest for Democratic Participation" Myrdal suggested that the vitality of the institutions of a welfare state depended on continued popular participation in their management and direction but that, paradoxically, the high degree of "created harmony" of interests which such polities attain has the effect of diminishing the impulse to such involvement. No problem without a solution: he called for government to do something about it. "The Welfare State," he wrote, "has to devote continual vigilance to the building up and preservation of its human basis." (A similar view was stated in 1965 by Henry C. Hart in a paper entitled "The Dawn of Community-Defining Federalism." He argued that the chief initiative and energy for such an effort would henceforth be coming from Washington.[30]) Analyzing the "special case of the United States," where democratic participation at all levels of government, as he saw it, was still far from satisfactory, perhaps least so of any of the Western democracies, Myrdal unerringly pointed his finger to the fact of ethnic diversity. "In spite of the very rapid advances made towards national integration, heterogenous elements still linger everywhere in the population, and with the remnants of separatistic allegiances."[31] With the rise of black nationalism in the 1960's ethnic hostilities assumed a singular intensity in the United States, and it may have seemed the quest for community was getting nowhere. Yet in one sense the Negro population could seem as evolving *towards* membership in the large national community *via* a stage of ethnic "separatistic allegiances."

In that sense, the community action programs of the war on poverty, with their singular emphasis on "maximum feasible participation" of the poor themselves comprise far the most notable effort to date to mount a systematic social response to this problem. As the work of social scientists and professional reformers, it must stand as a perceptive and timely initiative.

Perceptive for having got close to what would seem the heart of the matter; timely for having done so just a bit in advance of, but essentially in phase with, the emergence of much the same perception on the part of the public in general. A decade after Myrdal, James Q. Wilson, then emerging as one of the leading political scientists of the nation, reported on a research project conducted with his colleague and frequent collaborator Edward C. Banfield, which had sought to discover the terms in which urban residents perceived the "urban crisis" as it was uniformly designated at the time. A poll was taken among a sample of over one thousand Boston homeowners. The results were emphatic: [32]

The "conventional" urban problems—housing, transportation, pollution, urban renewal, and the like—were a major concern of only 18 per cent of those questioned, and these were expressed disproportionately by the wealthier, better-educated respondents. Only 9 per cent mentioned jobs and employment, even though many of those interviewed had incomes at or even below what is often regarded as the poverty level. *The issue which concerned more respondents than any other was variously stated—crime, violence, rebellious youth, racial tension, public immorality, delinquency. However stated, the common theme seemed to be a concern for improper behavior in public places.*

For some white respondents this was no doubt a covert way of indicating anti-Negro feelings. But it was not primarily that, for these same forms of impropriety were mentioned more often than other problems by Negro respondents as well. And among the whites, those who indicated, in answer to another question, that they felt the government ought to do *more* to help Negroes were just as likely to mention impropriety as those who felt the government had already done too much.

. . . What these concerns have in common, and thus what constitutes the "urban problem" for a large percentage (perhaps a majority) of urban citizens, is *a sense of the failure of community.*

Such information provides a direct clue to the difficulties encountered by the community action programs sponsored by OEO. Their tactics, when they became disruptive were presumably seen by the rest of the urban population as signs of the *further* deterioration of the community as a whole. What may or may not have been therapeutic for the poor was evidence to the nonpoor that the community was sicker than ever. This raises two further possibilities. Was the management of the program placed too much in the hands of young idealists suffused with what Norman Mailer terms the "middle-class lust for apocalypse" and altogether too little sensitive to the desire for order and respectable behavior by the great mass of the people who are simply neither rich nor poor? This was a time when the children of the more affluent middle class were going to considerable efforts to reject their heritage of liberalism and "nice things." A time when more than one prominent family could claim to have simultaneously one child in Haight-Ashbury and another in Bedford-Stuyvesant. On the other hand is this ever to be avoided? A related, and again unanswered question is whether the poor are ever to be politicized save in terms of conflict and fear and the creation of hate objects. Social science research has for decades established the high correlation between social class and the level of social participation: high-high, low-low. It may be that participation is more an effect than a cause, and that until there have been fundamental economic changes in the life of poor populations, these other qualities can only be achieved at the great costs in civility which Alinsky, nothing if not unflinching in his consistency and honesty, has repeatedly avowed. On the other hand, it would be a culture-bound absurdity to reject the possibility of evoking gallant and sustained public-regarding responses from the most deprived sectors of the population. The Left has much to answer for in American life, and not least for having

163

brought about a too ready rejection by men of the center of any assertion of proletarian cohesion and purpose. We have it from Oscar Lewis that Castro's Cuba solved the problem of juvenile delinquency by giving machine guns to its delinquents. Were the telescopic sights and mimeograph machines of the community action programs so very different? Whatever the case with each of these matters, the one compelling conclusion is that at no time were they sufficiently considered by the officials of the Federal government responsible for the program.

In his small book, *The Impact of the Social Sciences*, Kenneth G. Boulding speaks of the emergent style of social self-awareness:[33]

This movement of the social system into selfconsciousness is perhaps one of the most significant phenomena in our time, and it represents a very fundamental break with the past, as did the development of personal self-consciousness many millennia earlier.

Few more concrete instances of this slow transformation will be found in contemporary American government and politics than the emergence of the issue of participation, and it is almost wholly the work of social scientists and professional reformers.

It is also, of course, a flawed work. As much as its proponents can be said to have seized their opportunity, it may come to be judged that they also spoiled it. Their program survived, but only just, and it remains to be seen how much and for how long participation of the poor is truly tried. It remains to be seen whether it can do what is promised for it, just as we may discover to our sorrow that "participatory democracy" can mean the end of both participation and democracy. But the spirit of the times will not be stayed: these are the issues of this moment.

*NOTES*

1. Wofford, *op. cit.,* p. 11. It may be noted that earlier in the same paragraph he states, "We were looking for the bright generalist with an ability to negotiate, to review budgets, to know his own limitations, and to ask the right questions." But this becomes a "professional role."

2. *Nation's Business,* October 1967.

3. John G. Wofford, "Community Action; the Original Purpose," Social Sciences Forum, Adams House, Harvard University, Fall-Winter 1966–67.

4. *Op. cit.,* p. 599.

5. *Syracuse Post-Standard,* November 9, 1967. My italics.

6. *Wall Street Journal,* August 25, 1967.

7. *New York Times,* February 21, July 3, 1968.

8. Cited in Rubin, *op. cit.,* p. 12.

9. *Ibid.,* p. 11.

10. S. M. Miller and Pamela Roby, "The War on Poverty Reconsidered," to be published in Irving Howe and Jeremy Larner, *Poverty: Views from the Left* (New York: Morrill Publications, 1968).

11. *New York Times,* September 24, 1966.

12. *New York Times,* October 8, 1967.

13. George Nicolau, Address to the National Association for Community Development, Atlanta, April 8, 1968, mimeographed.

14. Wofford, *op. cit.,* p. 18.

15. *New York Herald Tribune,* April 15, 1966.

16. *New York Times,* November 5, 1965.

17. *New York Times,* November 6, 1966.

18. Blumenthal, *op. cit.,* p. 94.

19. In *Barron's National Business and Financial Weekly.*

20. *New York Times,* December 12, 1966.

21. Sar A. Levitan, "Lessons We Could Have Learned from the Antipoverty Efforts," mimeographed, 1967.

22. *New York Times,* June 28, 1968.

23. *New York Times,* March 15, 1967.

24. *New York Times,* April 10, 1967.

25. Richard W. Boone, "A Change in Structure," *New Generation,* Summer 1967.

26. Letter to the *New York Times,* May 15, 1967.

27. *New York Times,* July 24, August 18, October 14, 1967.

28. *Nation's Business,* October 1967.

29. In *Republican Papers,* ed. Melvin R. Laird, (Garden City, N.Y.: Anchor Books, 1968), pp. 171–190.

30. Henry C. Hart, "The Dawn of a Community-Defining Federalism," *Annals of the American Academy of Political and Social Science,* May 1965.

31. Gunnar Myrdal, *Beyond the Welfare State* (New York: Bantam Books, 1967), pp. 43–48.

32. James Q. Wilson, "The Urban Unease," *The Public Interest,* Summer 1968, pp. 26–27. (His italics.)

33. Kenneth Boulding, *The Impact of the Social Sciences,* Rutgers University Press, New Brunswick, 1966, p. 4.

# CHAPTER EIGHT

# *SOCIAL*
# *SCIENCE*
# *AND*
# *SOCIAL POLICY*

The object of this essay has been to chronicle in brief the introduction of a social science idea into a government program. That this was a not untroubled experience has hopefully been demonstrated. Yet different persons will likely reach quite disparate judgments as to what, even at this early date, can be learned. It may be hoped that when the essential facts of the experience are fully available, a more rigorous effort at judgment will be made. But it is to be doubted that it will. Or at least it would be unusual, as this kind of analysis does not attract a great deal of scholarly energy. (In the early planning of the Youth Employment Act, the main provisions of which became the Job Corps and the Neighborhood Youth Corps, the Department of Labor library searched in vain for a decent account of the great Civilian Conservation Corps of the New Deal.) Hence there may be some justification at this point in drawing such conclusions as can sustain the weight of such evidence as is available.

The first judgment, then, must be that during these years in Washington a good many men in the anti-poverty program, in and about the Executive Office of the President, and in the Congress, men of whom the nation had a right to expect better, did inexcusably sloppy work. If administrators and politicians are going to play God with other persons' lives (and still other persons' money), they ought at least to get clear what the divine intention is to be.

The essential problem with community action was that the one term concealed at least four quite distinct meanings: organizing the power structure, as in the Ford Foundation programs of Paul Ylvisaker; expanding the power structure, as in the delinquency program of Cloward and Ohlin; confronting the power structure, as in the Industrial Areas Foundation program of Saul Alinsky; and finally, assisting the power structure, as in the Peace Corps of Sargent Shriver. The task of government, in this case of the President's advisors, was first to discern these four different meanings, to make sure they were understood by those who had to make decisions about them, and to keep all concerned alert to the dangers of not keeping the distinctions clearly enough in mind. Which is not to say that policy had to choose between the various approaches: government no less than life is suffused with ambiguities and internal contradictions. But to be surmounted they must be perceived. *And there were warnings.* At a conference on Community Development held in San Juan in December 1964, while there was still time, the British social scientist Peter Marris outlined the contradictions between three of these views of community action. He proposed not to exclude any. He proposed that there be established in each community two organizations: one, close to city hall, for the purpose of studying and analyzing the local social structure, another for organizing the poor to bring their own strength to the bargaining table. It was abundant good sense, but ignored.[1]

Just possibly one reason is that the key decisions in the White House and the Executive Office of the President were made by lawyers and economists. None was especially familiar with the social science theory on which the various positions were based and, if an impression may be permitted, few were temperamentally attuned to the frame of mind of the reformers. Very possibly, a matter of professional style is involved here. William C. Mitchell has noted that "The political sociologist tends to view a political system as a place of *struggle* for power or influence, while the economist tends to see it as an essentially *cooperative* division of labor within which various forms and degrees of competition may take place for the various roles and rewards that constitute the system." Order and efficiency are the passions of lawyers and economists, and properly so. It may be that the presence is needed in the Executive Office Building of persons trained to other disciplines who can more readily give credence to the thought that there are those who with even greater passion seek disorder and destruction.

But this risks the tendentious: it was not social science competence that was missing in the conception and management of this program; it was intellect. By and large the political actors come off best. Their sensibilities quickly alerted them to the probability that the community action activists would cause more trouble than could be contained. Unfortunately, there was no creative political response forthcoming once this had actually begun to occur. The poorest perform-ance was that of the high-level staff aides, some nomi-nally political, some nominally in the career service, but far more like one another than otherwise, who busied themselves with the details of community action but never took time to inform themselves, much less their superiors, that the government did not know what it was doing.

This is the essential fact: *The government did not know what it was doing.* It had a theory. Or, rather, a set of theories. Nothing more. The U. S. Government at this time was no more in possession of confident knowledge as to how to prevent delinquency, cure anomie, or overcome that midmorning sense of power-lessness, than was it the possessor of a dependable formula for motivating Vietnamese villagers to fight Communism. At any time from 1961 to 1964 an after-noon of library research would have established that the Cloward-Ohlin thesis of opportunity structure, though eminently respectable, was nonetheless rather a minority position, with the bulk of delinquency the-ory pointed in quite a different direction. Nor would it have been necessary to have spent an afternoon to ascertain this not unimportant fact. Ohlin would have been pleased to make it explicit in the course of half an hour's conversation. Two practical considerations would have emerged from such a revelation. First, that most theorists in the field, because of their em-phasis on early family socialization, would be much less optimistic concerning rapid social change than were Cloward and Ohlin and their supporters. Much the same would be said of the Ford Foundation theory of institutional gymnastics: nothing seems to move that rapidly, at least in the view of most students of organizational behavior. Second, the divergence of the various theories was such that what would serve to cure in the one case would exacerbate in the other. A *big* bet was being made. No responsible persons had any business acting as if it were a sure thing.

In the work of Walter B. Miller, a comprehensive critique of the opportunity theory was to be found even before *Delinquency and Opportunity* appeared. In 1958, Miller reported the findings of a three-year study in a paper entitled, "Lower Class Culture as a Generating Milieu of Gang Delinquency." Miller's assertion —derived from meticulous field research—was that deviant behavior of delinquent youth was deviant only in the eye of the middle-class beholder, whereas for the young men involved, it was logical, utilitarian, everyday behavior, normal to a lower-class community.[3]

In case of "gang" delinquency, the cultural system which exerts the most direct influence on behavior is that of the lower class community itself—a long-established, distinctively patterned tradition with an intergrity of its own—rather than a so-called "delinquent subculture" which has arisen through conflict with middle class culture and is oriented to the deliberate violation of middle class norms.

He defined the "hard core" lower-class group primarily by its use of "female-based" households as childrearing units, and "serial-monogamy" as the basic childrearing unit. He explained the toughness of the young men, "the almost obsessive lower class concern with 'masculinity,'" as an adolescent device for acquiring male sexual identity in a female-based household. He insisted that the economy needs a lower class to provide low-skilled workers, and in effect maintains one for that purpose. He sensed that a settling down phase had begun.[4]

There is emerging a relatively homogeneous and stabilized native-American lower class culture; however, in many communities the process of fusion is as yet in its earlier phases, and evidences of the original ethnic or locality culture are still strong.

The essence of his position was that tastes differ, that lower class culture had a validity and integrity of its own and that, by implication, middle-class reformers should mind their own business.

Obviously Miller would not do. If middle-class reformers ceased to mind other people's business they would cease to be reformers. Their own opportunity structure would be artificially restricted; all manner of deviant behavior could be expected thereafter. Howsoever scientifically sound, Miller appeared to be politically conservative, and therefore, one is led to suspect, did not meet the needs of the private agenda of the middle-class reformers, namely, to prove a case against middle-class society. Years earlier, Joseph Schumpeter had argued that the great weakness of capitalism was in its inability to win the support of intellectuals. (Why is it totalitarian societies seem able to do so: or has this been only a twentieth century aberration?) Miller's formulations profoundly influenced sociological research during the early 1960's but were utterly excluded from influence on public policy.

In a thoughtful survey of sociological interpretations of delinquency, published in 1961, David J. Bordua provides both a critique of Cloward and Ohlin, and simultaneously suggests why the theory was so well adapted to liberal politics. He begins by describing the "classical" view of Frederick M. Thrasher, whose book *The Gang* appeared in 1927:[5]

The ecological processes which determine the structure of the city create the interstitial area characterized by a variety of indices of conflict, disorganization, weak family and neighborhood controls, and so on. In these interstitial areas, in response to universal childhood needs, spontaneous play groups develop. Because of the relatively uncontrolled nature of these groups—

or many of them at least—and because of the presence of many attractive and exciting opportunities for fun and adventure, these groups engage in a variety of activities, legal and illegal, which are determined, defined, and directed by the play group itself rather than by conventional adult supervision.

In *Delinquent Boys: The Culture of the Gang,* published in 1955, Albert K. Cohen took the quite different view that the lower-class youth acted as they did in order to restore the self-esteem that had been savaged by middle-class-dominated institutions, which constantly set them goals and standards they could not meet:[6]

The bulk of his basic viewpoint is the attempted demonstration that the common problem of adjustment of the lower class gang boys who are the carriers of the delinquent subculture derives from their socialization in lower class families and their consequent lack of preparation to function successfully in middle class institutions such as the schools.

The "middle-class measuring rod" was nonetheless applied to them; they would have to compete in a "democratic status universe" in which every boy could grow up to be President. To ease their own sense of failure in this universe, the lower-class youth set up their own "counterculture," which denies the validity of the middle-class measuring rod and sets up kind of an antinomianism among the select few of the Henry Street Gents, or whomever. To Cohen it looked like pointless, destructive, unavailing conduct.

Cloward and Ohlin rejected both Cohen and Miller. (The latter, as Bordua notes, is surprisingly reminiscent of Thrasher in his sense of the ecological basis of the behavior under discussion.) Where Cohen held that the delinquents accepted the judgment of the larger society, but devised means to avoid having to face those judgments. Cloward and Ohlin held that, to the contrary, "the delinquent norm systems are generated by boys who have already determined that their failures, actual or impending, are the fault of the larger social order." For what Bordua sees as "overwhelmingly polemical reasons," but which could just as easily relate to the private agendas of the authors, they are forced in the position of claiming that the delinquents' sense of injustice "must be objectively correct." Bordua finds this to be a serious failing.[7]

First, Cloward and Ohlin seem to be confusing the justificatory function of delinquent subcultures with their causation. All of these beliefs on the part of gang delinquents have been repeatedly reported in the literature, but, by the very argument of *Delinquency and Opportunity,* it is impossible to tell whether they constitute compensatory ideology or descriptions of objective reality.

Second, Cloward and Ohlin seem to be victims of their very general tendency to ignore the life histories of their delinquents. Thus, there is no way of knowing really what these subcultural beliefs may reflect in the experience of the boys. Third, and closely related to the ignoring of life history material, is the problem of assessing the degree to which these gang boys are in fact prepared to meet the formal criteria for success. To say that they are intelligent, strong, and agile is to parody the criteria for advancement. Perhaps Cohen would point out that intelligent, agile, strong boys who begin the first grade using foul language, fighting among themselves, and using the school property as arts and crafts materials do not meet the criteria for advancement.

It is quite true that  members of highly sophisticated delinquent gangs often find themselves blocked from whatever occupational opportunities there are, but this seems, often, the end product of a long history of their progressively cutting off opportunity and destroying their own capacities which may begin in the lower class family, as described by either Cohen or Miller, and continue through school failure and similar events. By the age of eighteen, many gang boys are, for all practical purposes, unemployable or need the support, instruction, and sponsorship of trained street-gang workers. Participation in gang delinquency in itself diminished the fitness of many boys for effective functioning in the conventional world.

If, indeed, Cloward and Ohlin mean to include the more attitudinal and characterological criteria for advancement, then it seems highly unlikely that any large number of boys trained and prepared to meet these demands of the occupational world could interpret failure exclusivley in terms which blame the system. They would have been too well socialized, and, if they did form a delinquent subculture, it would have to perform the psychological function of mitigating the sense of internal blame. This, of course, would make them look much like Cohen's boys.

In short, Cloward and Ohlin run the risk of confusing justification and causation and of equating the end with the beginning.

The most telling of Bordua's observations of Cloward and Ohlin is that their book contains only two references to the subject of family: one to say that it no longer conducts occupational training, the other to criticize Miller's views of the effects of female-based households. The delinquents described by other authors seemed to have had childhoods; they *grew* to be the way they were. "Cloward and Ohlin's delinquents seem suddenly to appear on the scene sometime in adolescence, to look at the world, and to discover, 'Man, there's no opportunity in my structure.'" Thus Bordua suggests that the Cloward and Ohlin position is best as a theory of "the origins of Miller's lower-class culture." Each generation goes through the same process of not meeting and not solving the problems of class structure barriers to opportunity. "This is why reform efforts can be so slow to succeed."

Could it not also, however, explain the peculiar attraction of the opportunity theory for reformers? It sweated earnestness, reeked of self-improvement. Could it be that where the Jewish scholars Cohen and Miller watched the antics of the *goyim* with wonder and detachment, the Protestants Cloward and Ohlin, suffering servants of the Lord, had to perceive in the whole miserable business the morally autonomous individual struggling for salvation? *Ha-mayvin yavin.* Bordua concludes his critique on a not entirely different note:[8]

All in all, though, it does not seem like much fun any more to be a gang delinquent. Thrasher's boys enjoyed themselves being chased by the police, shooting dice, skipping school, rolling drunks. It was fun. Miller's boys do have a little fun, with their excitement focal concern, but it seems so desperate somehow. Cohen's boys and Cloward and Ohlin's boys are driven by grim economic and psychic necessity into rebellion. It seems peculiar that modern analysts have stopped assuming that "evil" can be fun and see gang delinquency as arising only when boys are driven away from "good."

Not wholly. Analysts of great distinction, such as David Matza and Gresham M. Sykes, were willing at this time to describe delinquents in terms altogether reminiscent of those in which earlier ages depicted "bad" boys who need caning. They posit, for example, the process of "neutraliztion" whereby delinquents project blame on outside forces for propelling them into action or deny that any harm resulted from their acts. But if Miller would not do, certainly neither would Matza or Sykes.

Nor yet John H. Rohrer and Munro S. Edmonson. In their study *The Eighth Generation Grows Up,* a 1960 follow-up of Davis and Dollard's classic *Children of Bondage,* which appeared in 1940, Rohrer and Edmonson take the unequivocal position that the sources of gang delinquency lie in the early socialization of male children in a lower-class matriarchal home:[9]

The matriarchs make no bones about their preference for little girls, and while they often manifest real affection for their boy children, they are clearly convinced that all little boys must inexorably and deplorably become men, with all the pathologies of that sex. The matriarchal mother usually projects the blame for this result on the bad boys that lead her own little angel astray, and not infrequently attempts to counteract such influences with harsh if erratic punishments, but these frequently mast her own unconscious expectations of her son, and may do a great deal toward shaping him in the image of men she knows and approves or fears and represses. Whether the child actually contacts these men or not, such personifications have profound implications for his developing personality, especially in the first years of life. Whatever the influence of these aspects of the matriarchal climate, boys cannot learn to be men in a manless family, and we may assert unequivocally that this learning is institutionalized in the gang for most Negro boys of the lower class. . . .

Thus an organizational form that springs from the little boy's search for a masculinity he cannot find at home becomes first a protest against femininity and then an assertion of hypervirility. On the way it acquires a structuring in which the aspirations and goals of the matriarchy or the middle class are seen as soft, effeminate, and despicable. The gang ideology of masculine independence is formed from these perceptions, and the gang then sees its common enemy not as a class, nor even perhaps as a sex, but as the "feminine principal" in society. The gang member rejects this femininity in every form, and he sees it in women and in effeminate men, in laws and morals and religion, in schools and occupational striving.

Hypotheses: some developed very close to the subject at issue, others at some remove, all intelligent, well argued, well intended, but at very most only a tentative grasp on a fantastically elusive reality. Why then, it will be asked, did the social scientists involved in these events not insist on the limits of their knowledge and methodology. The answer would seem to lie in part in the essentially dual nature of the American social scientist. He is an objective "seeker after truth." But he is also very likely to be a passionate partisan of social justice and social change to bring it about. Herman Kahn has described the United States as "a white, Anglo-Saxon, Protestant, middle class, Christian-Fundamentalist country run by a coalition of minorities, which these terms do not describe."[10] By and large, social scientists would seem to have much more in common with those minorities than otherwise. Indeed increasingly they are not only personally drawn from them, in an ethnic and cultural sense, but make up a minority in their own right. During the 1960's, in particular, they have had quite extraordinary access to power. And they have used this access in considerable measure to promote social change in directions *they* deem necessary and desirable.

Noting the rise of the ideology of "participation" and

"social conflict," major themes in community action as it worked in practice, Irving Kristol observes that although its origins are complex, "obviously, it had more to do with an initial animus against the status quo than with any ripe sagacity about the difficulties of public administration in a large democracy."[11] This may be no more than to state that social scientists tend to be politically liberal or left, especially when they are young. Economists would seem to be rather an exception to this: as the discipline gets "softer," the radicalism grows more pronounced. Doubtless for the great bulk of sociologists and the like "extremism" takes no more extraordinary form than believing in civil rights for Negroes, but there is a gloss to these attitudes that in the circumstances of the 1960's would seem to have had enormous consequences. Social scientists love poor people. They also get along fine with rich people. (Not a few are wealthy themselves, or married to heiresses. In any event, in the 1960's, persons of great wealth have been a major source of support not only for social science research, but for radical political activity.) But, alas, they do not have much time for the people in between.

In particular, they would appear to have but little sympathy with the desire for order, and anxiety about change, that are commonly enough encountered among working-class and lower middle-class persons. The importance of Wilson's findings, cited earlier, is hardly to be overestimated. In the 1960's, the typical urban resident was himself growing more and more concerned about a "failure of community." But conceived not in the abstractions of a conservative philosopher such as Nisbet or an existential anarchist such as Goodman, but perceived in the same terms as the cop-on-the-beat: disorder. For whatever reasons, fundamental or transitory, justified or unjustified, "other" people did not seem to be behaving properly any longer, and the "typical" American grew more and more upset. During the 1960's, for the first time in the history of public opinion surveys, crime emerged as the principal issue of domestic concern.

The reaction among many of the more activist social scientists (obviously this risks labelling a vast number of persons from a smallish number of incidents) was not to be appalled by disorder, *but almost to welcome it.* How grand to live in interesting times! This began in earnest with the Negro riot in Watts in 1965, which was promptly declared not to have been a riot at all, but rather a revolt, an uprising, a manifesto, any term that suggested that the masses were on the move. For that love affair is still unrequited. Earlier, Midge Decter observed that the whole MFY enterprise reeked of the notion of the proletariat. This was especially to be seen in MFY's insistence that the "real" leaders of the people would not be the ostensible ones, that behind the institutional facade of political party committee-men, locality "mayors," vice lords, and parish priests, there was to be found an echelon of uncorrupted men who, given opportunity, would assume leadership and . . . what? Change the world.[12]

The presumption of superior empathy with the problems of the outcast is surely a characteristic, and a failing, of this liberal mindset. Thus in an otherwise helpful abstract on the "maximum feasible participation" clause Lillian Rubin writes that many of those involved in drafting the legislation seemed not to have understood its full meaning.[13]

A lifetime spent in an atmosphere dominated by racism and the casework emphasis of modern rehabilitation philosophy infects even the most sophisticated and sympathetic. It is difficult indeed to fully penetrate the stereotype—to envision and comprehend a poor man grasping abstract concepts of participation, a Negro asserting his manhood.

In illustration she cites a communication from James N. Adler, a young lawyer who worked with the Shriver task force.[14]

I had never really conceived [he writes] that it (participation) would mean control by the poor of the community action represented on the community action organization but that organization itself. . . . I expected that the poor would be such representation would be something in the order of 15 to 25% of the board. . . . *Moreover, I don't think it ever occurred to me, or to many others, that the representatives of the poor must necessarily be poor themselves.* [Her italics.]

One might think this a candid and helpful statement, coming, as it happens, from an unusually attractive and productive young political executive. But it was cited by Miss Rubin as a failure of imagination. In contrast with whom? Is a female graduate student in sociology at the University of California, Berkeley, better able to grasp the meaning of "a Negro asserting his manhood"?

All this might have been innocent enough, save that as the 1960's passed, signs increased that the various forms of public disorder either sanctioned, induced, or led by middle-class liberal-radicals had begun to acquire an ominous, even sinister cast in the mind of the public at large. At the necessary risk of oversimplification, it may be said that crime in the streets as a political issue began to assume the role that Communists in government had played in the 1940's and early 1950's. The parallels were striking: on the one hand an elite-proletarian axis, in which the proletarians played rather a passive role, or at least a largely non-ideological one, despite the interpretations to be read in the *Nation* or wherever. In between were the mass of fundamentalist citizens increasingly concerned, puzzled, and alarmed. The élite were in power; the fundamentalist *mass* out of power, save in institutions such as the Congress, the influence of which was largely negative. In particular, the élite controlled the major national institutions, such as the State Department in one era and the Department of Justice in the other, contrasted with the "mass" custody of such popular institutions as the police. In each instance the insistence by the fundamentalists was that something immediate be done; the response by the élite was that root causes must be attended to first. There was ethnic conflict: Catholic cops vs. Jewish radicals. There was regional conflict: New York and San Francisco vs. the Great Void, as the regions in between tend to be regarded at the extremities; the South, an ever-willing ally of the conspiracy hunters. There was the emergence of élite figures such as the Secretary of State and the Attorney General as symbols either of conspiracy or acquiescence in it. There was the control or near control of the national media by élitist journalists convinced that ultimate issues of liberty were at stake, and taking a not inconsiderable satisfaction in relating the ways of the Yahoos. There was the romanticization of the proletariat. Finally, the ambiguous role of the F.B.I., to which, mindlessly, the élite in both situations turned over custody of its most serious political problems. Deep wounds were inflicted by both sides as the tempo and intensity of conflict mounted, and community declined.

In both eras a distinctive posture of altogether too many members of the intellectual-academic world was to reject the legitimacy of the issue either of subversion or violence on grounds that those who raised it either were not intelligent enough to comprehend fully any complex issue or else had something other in mind than their putative concern for the public safety. The plain fact is that in both instances the intellectual group had acquired an *interest* in the political turmoil of the moment and came very near to misusing its position to advance that interest. In the first period the intellectual-academic community seemed filled with persons who, in Kristol's description, "prefer to regard Whittaker Chambers and Elizabeth Bently as pathological liars, and who believe that to plead the Fifth Amendment is the first refuge of a scholar and a gentleman.[15] In the second period the apologetics for violence were not less curious. The community action ideology became in ways more, not less, extreme in the face of evident failures. *Complete* community control, usually meaning black control, of all community-affecting institutions became the demand of the more militant whites. On the surface a reasonable enough position, in reality this took the form of denying the legitimacy of those institutions of electoral representation that had developed over the years—indeed, the centuries—and which nominally *did* provide community control. Of a sudden the city councilman was not enough, the state assemblyman not enough, the Congressman not enough, the mayor and the governor and the President but tools of the power structure. Plebiscitory democracy, the people-in-council, became the seeming nonnegotiable demand of many. The institutions of representative government, imperfect as they may be, have the singular virtue of defining who speaks for the community in certain set circumstances. Thus the elected (black) representatives of the Harlem community had several times ratified the construction by Columbia University of a gymnasium in Morningside Park. But the black students of the University decided that the assemblymen and senators, councilmen and borough presidents did not speak for the community, and that *they* did. This quickly enough becomes government, as one observer has noted, by a process of private nullification, which has never been especially good news for democracy. It would be absurd to blame the community action programs of the war on poverty for this *reductio ad absurdum,* but the legitimation of something called "community control," in opposition to the established system of electoral representation; the assumption that established systems were somehow not meeting the needs of the people, was certainly much encouraged by the community action movement. It is altogether natural that more conservative citizens became alarmed.

Nor is it to be wondered at that representatives of local government became concerned. In New York City the Republican John V. Lindsay had succeeded Wagner after a vigorous election campaign in which, generally speaking, he had adopted the radical critique of the antipoverty program, promising more participation, less control by City Hall. But in office, Lindsay, if anything, tightened control over such programs as he could get his hands on and evinced less and less enthusiasm for protesting welfare mothers and rampaging teen-age antipoverty program employees. Even the director of MFY indicated a measure of disenchantment. Far from insisting that the cure for participation was more participation, Beck and others like him became revisionists of sorts. The results of the "poverty elections" held in such places as Philadelphia and Los Angeles for representation on the local community action agency boards had been, as Wofford allows, pitiful. They appear to have made an impression on some persons at least. Early in 1968, Bertram Beck, Executive Director of MFY, spoke almost bitterly on the subject:[16]

To me, the great sell-out of the anti-poverty program was the invention of these elections of community corporations. There is a meager amount of money available. And where does it end up? It ends up with groups of poor people fighting one another over an inadequate, paltry sum of money that can do nothing. . . . It looks liberal. It looks great. It looks like a forward step. I say it's a regressive step.

Beck said more than that: in his view "too much antipoverty activity has been strictly agitational."

At this time, Lindsay proposed that community action agencies turn to more visible, tangible projects if they were to retain the confidence of the public and the Congress. In February 1968, he told a news conference, "Community action work in the past has tended to be in the field of community organization. But this must give way to the higher priority of public works type activity, particularly in the area of rehabilitation of physical structures." Mitchell Ginsberg, the City Human Resources Administrator, and an original board member of MFY, put it even more bluntly: "In the first stages all of the emphasis of the community action programs was on organization, but how many times can you organize the same people. You have to organize them to do something." Again, the flaws of the original antipoverty legislation were having their belated consequences: so much of the "hard" program having gone elsewhere, OEO and the community action programs were left with too little to do, and too much tendency to talk. Lindsay's private judgment may have slipped out six months later when, objecting to a Congressional move to transfer the Head Start program to the Department of Health, Education and Welfare, he said, "Head Start has been one of the few real successes of OEO."[17] But little came, at least in the short run, of his proposed redirection of community action. The City's Council Against Poverty would have to agree, and he indicated at the time that he was not sure it would. Many thought it was "demeaning" for the poor to work at such things as cleaning buildings, sidewalks, and vacant lots. Bertram Beck was appalled: "I don't see how we can expect the Mayor to run a city and an antipoverty program when he has such limited influence over it."

Thus the director of MFY was proposing powers for City Hall in 1968 that his predecessor had fiercely opposed in 1965. A learning process is to be observed: when the Johnson Administration put forth its Model Cities Program, it was provided that the communities involved would participate in the planning process, but strictly in association with the institutions of local government. "Somehow it has seemed easier," remarked H. Ralph Taylor, Assistant Secretary of Housing and Urban Development in May 1967, at a time the antipoverty program seemed almost lost, "to set up competing institutions than to make existing institutions work together more effectively." The political executives at HUD had no intention of letting happen to them what had happened to Shriver and his associates, and to their respective programs. Mayor Naftalin's quiet counsel was finally getting through.

The blunt reality is that sponsors of community action programs who expected to adopt the conflict strategy of Saul D. Alinsky and at the same time expected to be the recipients of large sums of public money, looked for, to paraphrase Jefferson, "what never was, and never will be." Alinsky emerges from the 1960's a man of enhanced stature. His influence on the formulation of the antipoverty program and its predecessors was not great. Indeed it was negligible, in that a primary motive of these efforts was to *give* things to the poor that they did not have. Alinsky's law, laid down in *Reveille for Radicals*, which appeared in 1946,[18] was that in the process of social change there is no such thing as give, only take. True or not, by the time the community action programs began to be funded, he had behind him some three decades of organizing poor or marginal neighborhoods (*white* as well as black) and in every instance this process had taken the form of inducing *conflict* and fighting for *power*. Was there not something to be learned here? Could it be that this is somehow the normal evolution once such an effort is begun? Was it not possible, for example, that MFY had to move towards disruption if those in charge of the program were to elicit any response from the neighborhood, and in that way acquire some feeling that they were having an impact? Alinsky's view was nothing if not explicit and public: social stability is a condition reached through negotiated compromise between *power organizations*. (His origins, of course, are in the trade union movement, specifically the United Mine Workers.) The problem of the poor is not only that they lack money, but that they lack power. This means they have no way of threatening the status quo, and therefore that there can be no social change until this organizational condition is changed. Organization first; antipoverty program second. Early in the life of the Office of Economic Opportunity, Alinsky was willing to contemplate that Federal funds, bypassing City Hall and channeled directly to indigenous organizations, might be used to bring such organizations into being. But his own experience and practice belied any such possibility. Throughout his career he had begun his organizing campaigns with cash in hand, completely independent of the power structure with which he wished to bargain. His entire analysis of the process of social change argued that official community action programs would soon fall under the direction of City Hall, as indeed they did.

Just as importantly, Alinsky (a "professional radical") posed a serious challenge to the concept of professionalism in reform. Speaking early in 1965, he used the analogy of the Foreign Aid program that had followed World War II. Why had the United States undertaken the program? From some moral principle? Nonsense. Foreign aid was begun because the Russians threatened. Precisely the same dynamics, he argued, would determine the outcome of the then barely begun war on poverty: "under present circumstances a poverty program based on a moral dynamism is not going to carry the thrust which comes from the threat" of an organized poor. The whole affair, he declared, was "political pornography," the first war ever launched on a balanced budget. He did not expect it would last long:[19]

Unless there are drastic changes in direction, rationale and administration, the anti-poverty program may well become the worst political blunder and boomerang of the present administration. If ever a program demanded an aggressive, partisan, unafraid-of-controversy administration it is the anti-poverty program. It must be a program which contends that poverty involves poverty of power as well as poverty of economy.

Whether or not his analysis was correct, his prognosis was near to perfect. It ought to have been attended to, but was not. One reason for this was the absence of persons within the administration attuned to such modes of thought, capable of assessing their validity, at very least, alert to the possibility that what such a man says might just be so.

The long-run effectiveness of Alinsky's organizing programs remains to be documented: the long-run has not yet occurred. But in the near-term, none can fault his insistence that social radicalism is not a civil service calling. Would it not, then, have been wiser for the antipoverty program to direct its efforts to the creation, for example, of trade union organizations in minority groups, using the contracting powers of the government and the protective sanctions of the National

Labor Relations Board to create units of economic and political power, which, once established, would thereafter have an independent life of their own? Was it that trade unionism had lost its glamor for the youth of the upper middle class who flocked to Shriver's OEO in the heady months of 1964 and 1965?

Similarly, would it not have been wise to seek ways to support and expand the activities of the small fundamentalist churches of the Negro community and the Pentacostal sects of the Puerto Ricans? Are these not the single incontrovertibly indigenous and independent institutions created by these minority slum dwellers in the present age? And are they not singularly vigorous and tough in the capacity to survive and to grow? Do they not *really* reflect the energies and personal styles of the poor? Or was it that hymn-shouting and bible-thumping somehow does not elicit in the fancies of the white radical quite the same fascination as does the black demi-monde? Difficult questions to answer, but ones appropriate to the calling and method of social science.

In sum, it must be insisted that the opportunity theory behind Mobilization for Youth is and was no more than that. Evidence to support it exists, but nothing like final agreement. To the contrary the theory of participation as therapy is much disputed. Bernard J. Frieden and Robert Morris write, in the context of the general problem of alienation: [20]

Least convincing have been those analyses which have asserted that the fact of participation by the poor, in itself, will significantly alter the conditions deplored, as for example the belief that civic participation in itself leads to a reduction in deviant behavior.

The failure of the social scientists, the foundation executives, the government officials lay in not accepting—not insisting upon—the theoretical nature of their <u>proposition</u>. As a matter for speculation, even for experiment, various forms of government-sponsored community action had much to commend themselves. The problems of community were properly a matter of concern at this time. But to proceed as if that which only *might* be so, in fact was so, was to misuse social science. It is the necessary condition of politics that action be based on insufficient knowledge. That is the responsibility of persons who get themselves elected as representatives of the people. They are expected, required, to act as if they know more than they do. Regularly they pay the price for turning out to have been wrong. Life in American politics is singularly solitary, nasty, brutish, and short—the exceptions only contrast with the generality—and those who with Hobbes would seek a "quiet corner" from which to observe it all, must deny themselves some of the excitements of the fray, or else not complain when bashed. One of the least attractive qualities of some of the early middle class practitioners of conflict-oriented community action was the tendency to cry "Foul" when the animal defended itself. Chazen, certainly a sympathetic commentator, writes:[21]

> The theoreticians were often unprepared for the enemies they acquired when their opinions of the public aid bureaucracy moved out of the professional journals and on to the picket signs. For an experienced labor or civil rights organizer there would be nothing unsettling about the political entanglements of militant social action. But social action enthusiasts came from an entirely different organizing tradition. Many of them arrived at their current welfare theories while organizing teenagers for juvenile delinquency projects which enjoyed the cooperation of city authorities. This preparation was not adequate for the political problems the social action theoreticians encountered when they obtained older constituencies in places like New York's Lower East Side.

Yet even he refers to Screvane as "Mobilization's executioner."

It is difficult to avoid the conclusion that in all these goings on social science was being misused. Professional persons were too willing by half to see public funds, and tax-free private funds, employed on a vast scale to further what was in effect a political agenda of a fairly small group of intellectuals. At just that time when their colleagues, and students, were raising the utmost rumpus about the intrusion of Federal money, and *therefore* influence into universities via national security and space programs, these professors were enthusiastically pressing for ever more public money to be expended in urban and rural neighborhoods in such a way as to change the political and social attitudes of the residents thereof. The precedent in either case is a questionable one. The next President of the United States as I write, will not be Lyndon Johnson. It could be George C. Wallace. How much public money would American liberals be willing to see President Wallace expend for the purpose of increasing the participation in public affairs of those elements in the population he regards as simultaneously deprived and underorganized? But this is an obvious point and need not be pressed, save to note that what is involved, in a word, is integrity. And common sense. If a populist, illiberal conservatism began swelling to ominous proportions in the late 1960's, the middle-class advocates of expressive violence and creative turmoil had something to answer for. Indeed it is directly to them, the professors and "pseudointellectuals," that Governor Wallace and others like him, addressed *their* critique of the power structure, and *their* challenge to the forms of civility and social stability that liberal academic America had seemingly thought so secure as not to need defending.

What then is to be said of the role of social science in social policy? Not, that is, of social scientists: a

teeming and irrepressible group, they will be on hand
proferring proposals for universal improvement doubtless for all time to come. And no bad thing. But this
they do in their capacity as citizens, as interested,
sentient beings. But is there something called social
science, a body of knowledge, a methodology that men
of quite disparate politics and temperaments will nonetheless agree upon, that can contribute to the formulation of public policy? I will propose that the answer
is a limited but emphatic Yes.

I have sought to argue, by illustration, that social
science is at its weakest, at its worst, when it offers
theories of individual or collective behavior which
raise the possibility, by controlling certain inputs, of
bringing about mass behavioral change. No such
knowledge now exists. Evidence is fragmented, con-
tradictory, incomplete. Enough snake oil has been sold
in this Republic to warrant the expectation that public
officials will begin reading labels. This precaution, if
growing, is nonetheless far from universal. In the late
1960's the circles in New York that a decade earlier
had conceived community action as a cure for delinquency, came forward with the notion that a slightly
different form would cure educational retardation on
the part of minority group public school children.
Community control *might* improve the school performance of slum children. It might *not*. No one knows.
It might have other effects that are quite desirable, *or*
undesirable. It is a perfectly reasonable proposal to try
out. But at this point in time it is almost unforgivable
that it should be put forth as a "proven" remedy for
anything. About the only forecast that could have
been made with any confidence would have been that
the effort to impose community control would lead to
a high level of community conflict, which in New York
City it has been doing, and which will presumably be
the case elsewhere.

191

This does suggest one area of social science usefulness. For while the reforming spirit is very much abroad in such circles, so also is the critical spirit, often creatively present in the same individual. Government, especially liberal government, that would attempt many things very much needs the discipline of skeptical and complex intelligence repeatedly inquiring "What do you mean?" and "How do you know?" The expectations of such government needs to be controlled by insights such as Nisbet's on the unlikelihood of final social peace:[22]

> The quest for community will not be denied, for it springs from some of the powerful needs of human nature—needs for a clear sense of cultural purpose, membership, status, and continuity. Without these, no amount of mere material welfare will serve to arrest the developing sense of alienation in our society and the mounting preoccupation with the imperatives of community. To appeal to technological progress is futile. For what we discover is that rising standards of living, together with increases in leisure, actually intensify the disquietude and frustration that arise when cherished and proffered goals are without available means of fulfillment. "Secular improvement that is taken for granted," wrote Joseph Schumpeter, "and coupled with individual insecurity that is acutely resented is of course the best recipe for breeding social unrest."

This will seem to some a formula for immobilism, but it is nothing of the sort. The two national political figures of the 1960's closest to the style and content of this tradition in social science thought have been John F. Kennedy and Eugene McCarthy. Both exceptionally creative innovators in politics. But both men whose minds were touched by a certain sadness at having perceived the complexity and difficulty of it all: both men for whom the achievement of limited goals lacked nothing in glory, as they knew all too well how problematic even that would be. Arthur M. Schlesinger, Jr., captured this quality with respect to Kennedy's seeming caution and seeming reluctance to move when all about him hot young blood demanded frontal assaults in all directions:[23]

I believe today that its basic source may have been an acute and anguished sense of the fragility of the membranes of civilization, stretched so thin over a nation so disparate in its composition, so tense in its interior relationships, so cunningly enmeshed in underground fears and antagonisms, so entrapped by history in the ethos of violence. . . . His hope was that it might be possible to keep the country and the world moving fast enough to prevent unreason from rending the skin of civility. But he had peered into the abyss and knew the potentiality of chaos.

The great failing of the Johnson administration was that an immense opportunity to institute more or less permanent social changes—a fixed full employment program, a measure of income maintenance—was lost while energies were expended in ways that very probably hastened the end of the brief period when such options were open, that is to say the three years from the assassination of Kennedy to the election of the Ninety-first Congress. In a sense, the repeated message of contemporary social science is that of the scarcity of social opportunity, rather as in earlier ages the scarcity of resources preoccupied the thoughts of economists. The consequence of such a sensibility is not so much great *caution*, as great *care*. Those who govern will do well to provide access for persons with such sensibilities: their views will commonly prove highly convergent with and congenial to the pragmatic liberal political mind that continues to provide much that is most to be valued in the American polity.

But this is a matter, primarily, of advice and counsel. What institutional role may the social sciences expect to play in public affairs. The answer seems clear enough. *The role of social science lies not in the formulation of social policy, but in the measurement of its results.*

The great questions of government have to do not

with what *will* work, but what *does* work. The best of behavioral sciences would in truth be of no very great utility in a genuine political democracy, where one opinion is as good as another, and where public policies emerging for legislative-executive collaboration will constantly move in one direction, then another, following such whim, fashion, or pressure that seems uppermost at the moment. What government and the public most need to know in the aftermath of this process is whether there was anything to show for the effort, and if so, what. Causal insights of the kind that can lead to the prediction of events are interesting, absorbing, but they are hardly necessary to the management of a large, open political system. All that is needed is a rough, but hopefully constantly refined, set of understandings as to what is associated with what. A good deal of medicine is no more than this, yet people are healthier as a result, and so might be the consequence for the body politic.

Perhaps the foremost example of this function to appear in the 1960's was the report on *Equality of Educational Opportunity*, known for its principal author James S. Coleman, which was issued by the U.S. Office of Education in 1966. Commissioned by Section 402 of the Civil Rights Act of 1964, the study began with a clear and untroubled understanding as to what the world was like. The U.S. Commissioner of Education was instructed within two years to report to the President and Congress "concerning the *lack* of availability of equal educational opportunities for individuals by reason of race, color, region, or national origin in public educational institutions." (My italics.) Two years later the second largest social science research project in history was released, almost furtively, by the Office of Education. The things "everybody knew" about education appeared from the massive collection of data—not to be so! School facilities were not especially unequal as between the races, and where differences did exist they were not necessarily in the presumed direction. In any event it did not appear that school facilities had any great influence on educational achievement, which seemed mostly to derive from the family background of the child and the social class of his schoolmates. The whole rationale of American public education came very near to crashing down, and would have done so had there not been a seemingly general agreement to act as if the report had not occurred. But it had, and public education will not now be the same. The relations between resource input and educational output, which all school systems, all legislatures, all executives have accepted as given, appear not to be given at all. At very least what has heretofore been taken for granted must henceforth be proved. Without in any way purporting to tell mothers, school teachers, school board superintendents what *will* change educational outcomes, social science has raised profoundly important questions as to what does not.

This hardly precludes experimentation. On the contrary, as techniques of evaluation evolve, outright laboratory-type investigations of social issues are likely to become more frequent, and certainly more useful. In 1967, for example, the Office of Economic Opportunity entered a $4 million contract with the Institute for Research on Poverty of the University of Wisconsin to carry out an experimental study of the effects of a negative income tax on one thousand low-income, intact, urban families in New Jersey, to extend over a period of fifty months. A generation ago such an undertaking would have seemed strange, if not outrageous. But the OEO announcement was accepted without apparent comment, perhaps especially owing to the professional reputations of the social scientists who would be engaged on the project. Quietly a new style in social innovation is emerging. The negative income tax project can be thought of in ways as a second generation of the PCJD "experiments." Much more money is available, more time, more expertise, or at all events more economists. In the judgment of Norton E. Long, who has looked into the matter, there would not appear to be much else to show for the delinquency programs. "The conduct of valid social science in hot policy areas," he writes, "is probably one of our society's prime needs." It did not come out of the PCJD, but OEO, that followed and continued the effort, and in terms that Norton would approve:[24]

The recommendation that would seem to follow from analysis of the materials is the necessity of separating research from the political action of innovation. The demonstration needs to be recognized as an attempt to influence which cannot be studied by those engaged in it, whose needs must be threatened by objective evaluation.

The circumstance of a University of Wisconsin team working in New Jersey would at least in part meet these terms. Similarly, OEO has engaged professional research organizations to evaluate some of its work, and these results have been of value. Thus a study of nine CAP's conducted in the winter of 1966–67 by Daniel Yankelovich, Inc., showed quite positive results for those individuals actually reached by the programs:[25]

The large majority of the poor reached by CAA programs report significant changes in their own and their children's lives as a result of their participation. For their children, they report improvements both in school and at home. For themselves, they report a mix of tangible and intangible benefits including new jobs, special training, more earnings, education, stretching available dollars further, improvement of neighborhoods, and increased hope, self-respect and confidence in the future (mixed with an intense impatience especially on the part of the Negro families to share in the affluence they see in the rest of the society.

A measure of reality testing would seem in order here: were the "reported" improvements, for example, observable to others besides those who reported them? Even so, the Yankelovich survey would suggest that community action agencies can produce results even if such do not always add up to social revolution. A similar set of enquiries might well be directed to the consequences of the abrupt discontinuation of efforts so hopefully begun. Was it the case, for example, that much of the discontent evident in Negro communities in the summer of 1967 was stirred by community action workers who either had been or were threatened with being *declassed* by cutbacks in the program?

Corresponding to the development of experimental technique in social innovation is the far more significant, if directly related, emergence of "social measurement," to use the term of John R. Meyer, as an area of special interest to social scientists, and in particular economists. On assuming direction of the National Bureau of Economic Research in 1968 Meyer reported the wide interest of his associates that "the Bureau in the 1970's should do for social statistics what it did for economic statistics in the 1930's."[26] With a sustained annual growth rate of 4 to 5 per cent in real national product seemingly increasingly feasible—that itself a tribute to the work of the Bureau—he asked whether it was not now time to turn the powerful methodology of modern economics to the analysis of social problems. "For example, have we come to a time when it makes sense to systematically document the status and changes in the status of the American Negro?"

Very much as the national government began compiling economic statistics that were to make economic planning feasible years before such planning became politically acceptable, the Federal establishment has for some time been expanding the collection of the raw social data to which Meyer proposes the new methodologies be directed. The Bureau of the Census, one of the truly noble institutions of the Federal government, has quietly been transforming its decennial survey into a continuous measurement process. Much room remains for improvement. (In 1960, some 10 per cent of the nonwhite population was missed, with proportions twice that and more among young adult males.) But there are not many mysteries left as to *how* to conduct an adequate census, and with more support the Bureau will be able to do just that. The truth of John Kenneth Galbraith's observation remains: statisticians are key actors in the process of social change, for it is often only when it becomes possible to measure a problem that it also becomes possible to arouse any political interest in solving it. For all its attentuated mandate, the provision of the Employment Act of 1946 committing the American national government "to promote maximum employment, production, and purchasing power" brought about the years of analysis that in turn led to the singularly successful political economy of the 1960's. With more foresight, might not a commitment to "maximum feasible participation" lead to a similar process of measurement and feedback? Something very like this has been proposed by Bertram M. Gross who was associated with the establishment of the Council of Economic Advisors, as was provided by the Employment Act. Responding to these initiatives, Senator Walter Mondale of Minnesota in 1967 introduced legislation, the Full Opportunity and Social Accounting Act of 1967, providing for the establishment of a Council of Social Advisors who would perform for the President, and the nation generally, the counterpart of the economists' role. Others have proposed that a social scientist be substituted for one of the three economists on the present council. The concept of a social report of the President, to parallel the economic report, has been widely discussed, and a group under the leadership of Daniel Bell began work on a proto-type. In 1966 Raymond A. Bauer and a group at the American Academy of Arts and Sciences published a group of papers under the heading *Social Indicators* which marked the beginning of systemic inquiry into the issue.

The potential of these proposals is easily underesti-mated, as are the dangers implicit in some of the present trends in social measurement. The demands of rational resource allocation, so compelling on so many grounds, have already led to an extensive de-velopment of "social measurement" techniques in the executive branches of American government, especi-ally the Federal government. This very largely is what the renowned, if somewhat over-touted Program Plan-ning Budgeting System (PPBS) represents, a system largely developed in the Defense establishment and under Johnson colonized throughout the Federal es-tablishment. Should this trend continue, and it will, the result will be a considerable exacerbation of a situation already to be observed, namely, a pronounced and growing imbalance between the "knowledge" as to what works and what does not, what is needed and what is not, available to the executive branch of gov-ernment, as against the legislature. In hearings before the Subcommittee on Executive Reorganization of the U. S. Senate Committee on Government Operations in December 1966, I had occasion to comment on this development in terms that seem relevant here:

There is nothing sinister about this state of affairs. Serious evaluation research is only just approaching the state of a de-veloped, as against an experimental, technique. Inevitably it

has been sponsored in the first instance by executive departments. However, precisely because the findings of such research are not neutral, it would be dangerous to permit this
imbalance to persist. Too often, the executive is exposed to the
temptation to release only those findings that suit its purposes;
there is no one to keep them honest. Similarly, universities and
other private groups which often undertake such research on
contract are in some measure subject to constant, if subtle,
pressure to produce "positive" findings. The simple fact is that
a new source of knowledge is coming into being; while it is
as yet an imperfect technique, it is likely to improve; and if
it comes to be accepted as a standard element in public dis-
course it is likely to raise considerably the level of that dis-
course. This source of knowledge should not remain an executive monopoly.

What is to be done? I would offer a simple analogy. In the
time this nation was founded, the principal form in which
knowledge was recorded and preserved was in printed books,
and accordingly in 1800 Congress established the Library of
Congress as a source of information. Over the next century,
techniques of accounting and budgeting developed very
rapidly, and in 1921 Congress established the General Accounting Office to keep track of federal expenditures. I would like
to suggest that Congress should now establish an Office of
Legislative Evaluation in the GAO which would have the task
of systematically reviewing the program evaluations and
"PPBS" judgments made by executive departments. This office
would be staffed by professional social scientists. On occasion
they would undertake on their own to assess a Federal program, jut as on occasion the GAO does an audit of its own;
but in general their task would be to "evaluate the evaluators"
and in this way both maintain and improve the quality of the
regular ongoing work of the executive departments in this
field, and also routinely make these findings available to the
Congress. It should not be expected that their findings will be
dramatic or that they will put an end to argument—just the
contrary is likely to occur. But the long-run effect could be
immensely useful, if only because Congress would have some
clearer idea than it now has as to what it is doing.

Some will feel that the very existence and distribution of
knowledge of this kind is a threat to continued experiment and
innovation. I disagree. I would argue, for example, that the
General Accounting Office has in its 45 years of activity raised
the level of financial honesty in the programs of the Federal
government to the point that it is no longer even a remote
obstacle to federal legislation. Federal money may get wasted,
but it rarely gets stolen. The American people know this, and

I am persuaded that it profoundly affects their willingness to pay taxes for the support of federal programs. I believe further that if we began to be as careful and as open about assessing the results of social programs as we are in ensuring the personal honesty of those involved with running them, we might begin to see a more enduring willingness to keep trying—as well, perhaps, as a welcome reluctance by cabinet officers to "oversell" their program to begin with.

We have set ourselves goals that are, in some ways, unique in history: not only to abolish poverty and ignorance, but also to become the first genuinely multi-racial and, we hope, in the end non-racial democracy the world has seen. I believe that in moving toward these goals, and in seeking to change the present reality, an unflinching insistence on fact will be a major asset.[27]

And there is an issue beyond objectivity. The "movement of the social system into self-consciousness" has been accompanied by increasingly sophisticated efforts to shape and direct that system. Increasingly social scientists are recruited for such attempts; increasingly they themselves initiate them. There arises then a range of questions of ethical behavior that correspond to the canons of professional practice with respect to individual clients. Social workers have developed, and in some cases borrowed from other professions, a quite extensive set of rules governing and protecting professional conduct. They can for example, purchase insurance for suits against malpractice. *But what is malpractice with respect to a community?* At what point are risks taken that are not justified? In what way is it to be determined whether advice was incompetent or treatment negligent? Difficult, perhaps unavailing questions. But questions withal. A generation ago Reinhold Niebuhr forewarned us that the major difficulty of our time would be that of imposing ethical standards on the behavior of large organizations, an effort suddenly imposed on society after three millenia of slowly developing standards of personal conduct. Rather the same challenge faces those who would "engineer" social change. The problem goes beyond individual measures of professional competence to the question of the very possibility of such competence. Looking back it is clear, for example, that the community action programs of the war on poverty lent themselves to a rise in internal domestic tensions only in part because of their intrinsic qualities, and far more because of a rise of upper middle class white disaffection with the direction of American society occurring in conjunction with an even more powerful surge of the civil rights movement associated with an inevitable, and in ways much overdue rise of militant black assertiveness. Had these developments been foreseen it may well be that wisdom in government would have dictated another course for the antipoverty program, there having developed on its own an altogether sufficient potential for community activism. Prescriptions for arousing the "silent" students and inert mass as of the Eisenhower era, may only have exacerbated the tendencies of the period of the Students for a Democratic Society and the Black Panthers. But who was to know this would be the case? Exactly. It was not possible to know: it *is* not possible. Wisdom surely bespeaks moderation in projections of the future, and restraint in its promises for it.

This is, of course, first of all a challenge for those who practice the most demanding calling of all, that of government itself. For them, Edmund Burke's conception of successive generations as possessing their society's laws and customs of governance in the form of an entailed estate, given them for lifetime use, with the condition that it be passed on at least not diminished and hopefully enhanced, seems especially relevant now in the United States. The 1960's, which began with such splendid promise of a new and higher unity for the nation, are ending in an atmosphere of disunity and distrust of the most ominous quality. For it is not the old and weak and excluded who have been illused, or think themselves such. Rather it is the vibrant, established, *coming* young people of the nation who in large numbers have learned to distrust their government, and in many ways to loathe their society. They are not yet in power. *They will be.* When that day comes, however moderated their views may have become, their understanding of their country will have been shaped by the traumas of the 1960's. Not least of these shocks has been the debacle of the community action programs of the war on poverty: the soaring rhetoric, the minimum performance; the feigned constancy, the private betrayal; in the end, to their understanding, the sell-out. All this will be part of a past that has already shaped the future. It will then be asked, by some at least, how well the men who held office in that near to heartbreaking decade exercised their brief authority.

*NOTES*

1. Peter Marris, "The Strategies of Reform," Conference on Community Development, San Juan, Puerto Rico, December 1964, mimeographed. Marris probably would not see the "Peace Corps model" as a distinct variety of community action.

2. William C. Mitchell, "The Shape of Political Theory to Come," *American Behavioral Scientist*, November-December 1967, p. 16.

3. *Journal of Social Issues*, XIV (1958).

4. Walter B. Miller, "Implications of Urban Lower Class Culture for Social Work," *The Social Service Review*, September 1959, p. 225.

5. Frederick M. Thrasher, *The Gang* (Chicago: University of Chicago Press, 1927).

6. Albert K. Cohen, *Delinquent Boys: The Culture of the Gang,* (New York: The Free Press, 1963).

7. Richard A. Cloward and Lloyd E. Ohlin, *Delinquency and Opportunity: A Theory of Delinquent Gangs* (New York: The Free Press, 1960).

8. David J. Bordua, "Delinquent Subcultures: Sociological Interpretations of Gang Delinquency," *Annals of the American Academy of Political and Social Sciences,* 338 (November 1961), 119 ff. Bordua is at pains to note the difficulties of correctly, adequately compressing complex positions, and I, of course, have compounded the likelihood of distortion by compressing him. It is done, however, solely to illustrate the uncertainties of the theoretical position which the government adopted. I have not discussed the immensely interesting findings of the Cornell Program in Social Psychiatry concerning the influence of community organization on an impoverished community in the Maritime Provinces of Canada, as this material was not generally available in the early 1960's. However, the concept of "poverty in a context of social disintegration" associated with A. H. Leighton clearly has much bearing on this subject, and very much supports the thesis that some form of community organization is needed. See Alexander H. Leighton, "Poverty and Social Change," *Scientific American,* May 1965; Morton Beiser, "Poverty, Social Disintegration and Personality," *The Journal of Social Issues,* January 1965. For data disputing the common-value system posited by Merton, see Herbert H. Hyman, "The Value Systems of Different Classes: A Social Psychological Contribution to the Analysis of Stratification," in Reinhard Bendix and Seymour Martin Lipset, eds., *Class, Status and Power* (New York: Free Press, 1953), pp. 426–442. Cloward and Ohlin's relative disinterest in family socialization would, of course, reflect the influence of Durkheim, whose views in such matters are very much in contrast to those of Freud. Marc Fried writes: "Durkheim self-consciously set himself the task of developing a field of sociology and rejected the fundamental *theoretical* importance of psychological factors as basic, explanatory variables.*** In effect, Durkheim points out that individual behavior is the individualized expression of socially determined tendencies." Fried has, with some success, argued that "only a slight shift in perspective" will reveal the contrasting positions of Freud and Durkheim as formulations of a *"complementary relationship between the individual and his society."* Durkheim's views are in general more hospitable to government action, certainly of government sponsored *reform,* than Freud's gloomy insistance on self-denial and repression as the condition of civilization. See Marc Fried, "Social Problems and Psychopathology" in *Urban America and the Planning of Mental Health Services.* Group for the Advancement of Psychiatry, New York, 1964.

9. John H. Roherer and Munro S. Edmonson, eds., *The Eighth Generation Grows Up* (New York: Harper Torchbooks, 1960), pp. 161–63.

10. Herman Kahn, "Truce or More War?" *U.S. News & World Report,* June 3, 1968.

11. Irving Kristol, "Decentralization for What?" *The Public Interest,* Spring 1968, p. 20.

12. See Daniel P. Moynihan, "Three Problems in Combatting Poverty," in Margaret S. Gordon, ed., *Poverty in America* (San Francisco: Chandler Publishing Company, 1965).

13. Rubin, *op. cit.,* p. 9.

14. *Ibid.*

15. Irving Kristol, "The Web of Realism," *Commentary,* June 1964, p. 610.

16. Bertram Beck, Remarks, New York Report, WOR-TV, February 11, 1968.

17. *New York Times,* July 27, 1968.

18. Saul D. Alinsky, *Reveille for Radicals,* Chicago, Ill., University of Chicago Press, 1946.

19. Saul D. Alinsky, "The War on Poverty Political Pornography," *The Journal of Social Issues,* January 1965.

20. Bernard J. Frieden and Robert Marris, *Urban Planning and Social Policy* (New York: Basic Books, 1968), p. 178. But see also Erdman B. Palmore and Phillip E. Hammond, "Interacting Factors in Juvenile Delinquency," *American Sociological Review,* December 1964, pp. 848–854.

21. Chazen, *op. cit.,* p. 608.

22. Nisbet, *op. cit.,* p. 73.

23. Arthur M. Schlesinger, Jr., *A Thousand Days* (Boston: Houghton Mifflin Company).

24. Robert K. Merson, *Social Theory and Social Structure,* rev. ed. (New York: The Free Press, 1957), p. 3.

25. "Detailed Findings of Study to Determine Effects of CAP Programs on Selected Communities and Their Low Income Residents," prepared for Office of Economic Opportunity, Daniel Yankelovich, Inc., March 1967, pp. 8–9.

26. John R. Meyer, "The National Bureau: Continuity, Change and Some Future Perspective," Toward Improved Social and Economic Mesaurement, Forty-eighth Annual Report, National Bureau of Economic Research, Inc., 1968, p. 1.

27. Daniel P. Moynihan, "A Crisis of Confidence?" *The Public Interest,* Spring 1967, pp. 9–10, adapted from Testimony given before Subcommittee on Executive Reorganization, Committee on Government Operations, *Federal Role in Urban Affairs,* December 13, 1966.

# INDEX

```
  203
   12
 ─────
  215
```

```
        30     FINISH TUESDAY
   7/215
     21
   ─────
      5
```

```
          203
          130
        ─────
           73
```